# MY INGLISH KITCHEN

MALISHA NICHHABHAI

Clink Street

*Published by Clink Street Publishing 2024*



*First edition.*



*ISBN:*
*978-1-913568-63-4 - hardback*
*978-1-913568-64-1 - ebook*

# CONTENTS

## SALADS AND PICKLES



## RAITA'S, DIPS AND CHUTNEY'S



## SWEET TREATS



## SNACKS AND NIBBLES



## DRINKS

# A LITTLE ABOUT ME

This book is dedicated to my mum and dad for the lifelong inspiration they have given me to become the cook I am today; my supportive husband who has given me the confidence to write this book so families like ours can create and enjoy the delicious food that we eat; and lastly, my 3 beautiful children who make it all worth being me. I love you all always.

I am a UK born Hindu. My mum was born in the UK too, in fact my mum and I were born in the same hospital, Preston Royal. She lived here until her teens before the whole family moved back to Gujarat, India. Many years later she met my dad. After tying the knot, my mum moved back to the UK with my dad in the early to mid 80's. That's when my younger sister and I were welcomed into the world.

Having married a Yorkshire man, I now live in Huddersfield with my husband and 2 beautiful young daughters and baby boy.

When my parents settled in Manchester, they brought with them a treasure of culture and heritage, including the Indian Gujarati cuisine. My cooking is a combination of my parents' nurturing and teaching. With my mum being British born and having lived the first half of her childhood in the UK, her cooking also has many British influences, which my dad can't understand because he's a proper Indian through and through. I love this about him though because his culture and morals alway kept us grounded. My mum was never expected to do all the cooking. Especially at weekends, I loved how they would both cook together in the kitchen. Growing up I watched them cook and I became inquisitive with their culinary approaches and techniques to cooking. This, coupled with a lifetime of non Indian influences and experiences from being born in the UK, made me the home cook that I am today. I'm extremely grateful and proud of my heritage and upbringing. I'm very lucky to have been brought up with open minded parents who gave me the opportunity to have a modern yet cultured life.

When I cook for my family now I want to cook them a dish that's not only nutritious but a satisfying home cooked meal.

I was taught the basics of Indian cooking from my parents. My mum is the expert when it comes taste. Her food is simple, elegant and effortless. She would still to this day happily cook for a guest party of 15-20 people with zero stress and zero sweat. On the other hand my dad was the experimenter with his cooking. I remember sometimes I would see my mum looking at my dad thinking what is he doing, that's not right? But with my dad there was no right or wrong when it came to cooking and new creations. You would never quite know what to expect when he was in the kitchen. Nonetheless he'd always create a culinary masterpiece.

As an Indian my mum would always complain to my dad saying that I needed to master and learn to cook several dishes before my time came to get married. My dad was very soft with us and always replied to her saying that we had our whole life to learn, and that we should enjoy our life before we get married. I obviously agreed with him. He was more interested in us having a good education and building long standing careers rather than becoming domesticated housewives.

Then I got married to a Yorkshire man, and wow, marriage taught me that there was way more to learn. Although my family ate meat, we were predominantly vegetarians throughout the week and carnivores at the weekend. My in-laws were very different. They ate a mixture of veg and non veg throughout the week. I still remember the first time I met my mother in law when I started dating my husband. She was making chicken biriyani, I thought I'd give her a hand and get on her good side. She had boiled eggs for the biriyani and asked me to peel off the shell. Well I had never cooked an egg in my life, let alone peel the shell off. My dad didn't like the smell of cooking eggs, so we never had eggs in the house. I looked at the eggs and my mother in law could see the confusion on my face. She was kind and showed me how to do it. All I had to do was roll the egg on the work surface to crack the shell then peel. It was that simple.

My biggest culinary inspiration is my mum. I feel like I will never stop learning from her. With the experience and knowledge she has passed on to me, I have become the cook I am today. I am able to feed my family the same nutritious and exciting food that I was brought up with.

With the young family I have I am continuously adapting the food I cook to suit their ever evolving taste buds.

Food is the centre point of our family. Whether it's just the 5 of us or entertaining guests, we are always in the kitchen together at meal times.

Meal times means family time. It's the most precious part of the day for me. We are all so busy during the day with work, school and activities, that I look forward to this special time everyday. Both my husband and I will cook, but generally it's me because I love being in the kitchen and I love to feed my family. It is absolute chaos when all 5 of us are in the kitchen but I wouldn't have it any other way. While I'm cooking away, my husband is the one who will ensure that we both have a well deserved drink in our hand whilst also entertaining our 3 little munchkins. Basically I'm the cook and he's the entertaining bartender.

Being a busy working family, I try to prep as much as I can to ensure my family are eating wholesome and nutritious home cooked food throughout the week. I'd love to cook fresh food daily, but realistically which working family has the time to do that? So I do batch cook where possible, and freeze for those days when everything else in life takes over.

This book is full of heart warming memories of my childhood and all the food that I now love to cook and eat with my family. I always cook the same meal for us all and leave out the spiciness for the children. Whether you have children or not, all my recipes are adaptable to suit all ages and diets.

The food in this book is a celebration of life, and that is exactly what this book will bring you.

I hope you enjoy this book as much as I enjoyed writing it for you.

Love Malisha.

# SPROUT YOUR OWN LENTILS

Make your own sprouted lentils or mung beans, in this case, by washing them in water until the water runs clear. Give one final rinse in warm water and soak for 24 hours. After this time has passed you will see the mung beans' skin has cracked and that theylook plump. Drain the water. Wash the mung in clean warm water and drain. Line a large colander with kitchen tissue and scatter the lentils into the colander. Cover with kitchen tissue and leave for 24 hours at room temperature. Trickle water over the kitchen tissue and leave for a further 24 hours. If you find they haven't fully sprouted after the 48 hours have passed, then leave for another day if necessary. Once sprouted you can store in the fridge for up to 3 days, ready to eat. Add to your stir fries and salads.

# GINGER, GARLIC AND GREEN CHILLI PASTES

The holy trinity for everyday cooking – garlic, ginger and green chilli pastes form the basis for most Indian recipes. In my kitchen I use one or the other, or all three in almost every dish I make. Not only do these 3 key ingredients add a depth of flavour and aroma, each boasts various health benefits, from helping with digestion to fighting flu and lowering blood sugar levels. I love making my own homemade pastes for ease and convenience of everyday cooking, instead of chopping and blending from scratch every day. These pastes stay fresh in the fridge for up to 2 weeks!

## METHOD

Simply peel and blend 250g ginger with ½ tbsp of avocado oil until they form a paste. Store in an airtight container in the fridge.

Use the same process to make the garlic paste and green chilli paste. 250g of peeled garlic with ½ tbsp of avocado oil or 250g of green chillis with ½ tbsp of avocado oil.

Happy Cooking!

# VEGETARIAN

# PANEER MASALA

A delicious and comforting paneer masala dish that is the ultimate vegetarian comfort food. This decadent curry is simple to put together and is a great curry fix. Made with onion, tomato, ginger-garlic paste, and aromatic spices. Whole spices are used to make this super delicious dish, which lends it a beautiful aroma along with flavour. It is delectably rich, and pairs well with almost all Indian bread, especially with naan. I sometimes even serve it with Jeera Rice.

**SERVES 4**

## INGREDIENTS

### Paneer marinade

- *400g paneer, cut into 2cm cubed pieces*
- *3 tbsp sunflower oil for shallow frying*
- *¾ tsp salt*
- *¾ tsp red chilli powder*
- *¾ tsp turmeric*

### Whole spices

- *2 green cardamom pods*
- *6 black peppercorns*
- *1 piece cinnamon stick*
- *4 cloves*

### Masala gravy base

- *2 medium onions, roughly blended*
- *4 medium tomatoes, roughly blended*
- *3 tbsp sunflower oil*
- *200ml warm water*
- *1 tsp ghee*
- *2 dried Kashmiri red chillies*
- *2 green chillies, slit in half lengthways*
- *½ tsp cumin seeds*
- *2 tsp garlic paste*
- *2 tsp ginger paste*
- *2 tsp coriander powder*
- *½ tsp cumin powder*
- *¾ tsp turmeric powder*
- *2 tsp red chilli powder*
- *1 tsp garam masala*
- *1 tsp salt, or to taste*
- *1 tbsp lemon juice*
- *2 tbsp kasuri methi (dried fenugreek leaves)*
- *Chopped fresh coriander for garnish*

## METHOD

Soak the paneer in warm water for 5 minutes. Drain and pat dry. Marinate the cubes of paneer in the salt, red chilli powder and turmeric. Coat each piece evenly. Set aside for 20 minutes.

Shallow fry the paneer in 3 tbsp of sunflower oil until all sides are golden in colour. Drain any excess oil on kitchen paper and set the paneer to one side.

Now using a pestle and mortar, grind the whole spices listed. Set the crushed whole spices to one side.

Now you can prepare the gravy base.

In a heavy bottom wide saucepan, heat the sunflower oil and ghee on medium heat. Add the dried Kashmiri red chillies and the crushed whole spices. Swirl around in the oil and ghee until they release a beautiful aroma.

Now add the grated onions and sauté on a low heat until caramelised and golden.

Now add the garlic paste and ginger paste. Mix well with the onions and sauté for a further 2 minutes.

Add the turmeric powder, cumin powder, coriander powder, garam masala, green chillies and salt. Combine all the spices well with the onion mix. Cook for 2 minutes.

Now add the grated tomatoes, mix well and cook for 10 minutes until the oil starts to separate from the edges of the masala mix.

Add 200ml of warm water, stir through and simmer on a low heat for 10 minutes. Now add the fried paneer and cook for a further 5 minutes.

Finally add the kasuri methi and the lemon juice. Stir through and take off the heat. Garnish with fresh coriander and serve with naan or jeera rice.

# INDIAN SPICED BRUSCHETTA

This dish is a spicy twist to the traditional bruschetta. An Indian influence that is aromatic and delightful with the right balance of spicy flavours. Makes great finger food for picnics, gatherings, or simply lunch.

**SERVES 2**

## INGREDIENTS

- *4 slices sourdough from baguette, brushed with extra virgin olive oil*
- *200g cherry tomatoes, quartered*
- *1 medium red onion, finely chopped*
- *3 tbsp finely chopped coriander*
- *Juice of ¼ lemon*
- *¾ tsp cracked black pepper*
- *½ tsp salt, or to taste*
- *½ tsp red chilli flakes*
- *½ tsp toasted cumin seeds*
- *Pinch of dry pomegranate (Anardana)*
- *2 tsp extra virgin olive oil*
- *Basil for garnish*
- *Garnish with crumbled paneer*

## METHOD

Firstly, on a hot griddled pan, lightly griddle both sides of the sourdough brushed with extra virgin olive oil. Set aside.

Prepare the bruschetta topping by adding the quartered cherry tomatoes to a large mixing bowl along with the chopped red onion, coriander, lemon juice, black pepper, salt, red chilli flakes, toasted cumin seeds, anardana and olive oil. Mix and combine all the ingredients together well.

Top your toasted sourdough with the bruschetta topping.

Crumble over the paneer and garnish with fresh basil and serve!

# MASALA EGGY BREAD

If you want a quick and easy brunch option, my masala eggy bread is just the thing. In my house we call this egg dip and the kids love it without the spice, so make sure you adapt the spice level for this recipe to suit the family.

**SERVES 2**

## INGREDIENTS

- *4 thick slices of bread*
- *4 large eggs*
- *1 tsp milk*
- *Salt and pepper, to taste*
- *2 tsp chilli flakes*
- *2 tbsp finely grated mild cheddar*
- *1 tbsp parmigiano-reggiano*
- *Half red onion, finely chopped*
- *1 tomato, deseeded and finely chopped*
- *2 tbsp finely chopped coriander*
- *Butter for cooking*

## METHOD

Whisk the eggs in a large bowl and add the milk.

Add the remaining ingredients (apart from the bread) and whisk together.

Dip a slice of the bread into the eggy mixture and coat both sides of the bread well.

Place a frying pan on medium heat and add a small knob of butter. Just as it melts, place the eggy bread into the pan and cook on a medium heat for approx. 3 minutes on each side, until the cheese starts to crisp.

Serve while it's warm. Go on make yourself a cup of chai too.

CHILLI CHEESE BHAJIA

# CHILLI CHEESE BHAJIA

My super easy bhajias are made from gram flour, red onions, carrots, peas and grated mild cheddar. Spiced with chopped green chillies, garlic, ginger and chilli powder. They are so moreish. I normally eat the first batch with the kitchen door closed. Goes down a treat with the kids too (minus the chilli). The perfect snack for a lazy Sunday afternoon.

**SERVES 4**

## INGREDIENTS

- *200g chickpea flour*
- *1 large finely chopped red onion*
- *1 large finely chopped carrot*
- *2 tbsp of petit pois*
- *1 tsp red chilli powder*
- *4 birds eye green chillies, finely chopped*
- *¼ tsp turmeric*
- *1 tsp salt, or to taste*
- *100g grated mild cheddar*
- *½ tsp garlic paste*
- *1 tsp ginger paste*
- *2 tbsp sunflower oil, plus extra for deep frying*
- *100ml water*
- *4 tbsp breadcrumbs*

## METHOD

In a large mixing bowl add the chickpea flour and 2 tbsp sunflower oil, combine and mix.

Add the remaining ingredients to 100ml of water. The batter should thicken and stick to your fingers.

On a low heat add sunflower oil in a deep frying pan/wok for deep frying. Heat to 180 degrees.

Using a tbsp, scoop dollops of the batter into the hot oil. Do not overcrowd the pan by frying too many at once as this will reduce the temperature of the oil. Fry 3-4 at a time dependent on the size of your pan. Using a slotted spoon turn the bhajias in the oil frequently to evenly cook on all sides. Once they are beautifully golden on all sides remove from the oil and drain on tissue paper.

Serve whilst they are fresh and warm with a condiment or chutney of your choice.

DILL MUTHIA (DILL DUMPLINGS)

# DILL MUTHIA (DILL DUMPLINGS)

They are called muthia because they are shaped using your fist. The dumplings are shallow fried until crisp and golden on the outside but still soft in the middle. This is one I remember well from my younger days. Weekend breakfasts would always consist of my mum making these to dip into my morning chai.

**SERVES 4**

## INGREDIENTS

- *40g fresh dill*
- *175g juwar flour (sorghum flour)*
- *175g chickpea flour*
- *2 tbsp yellow course semolina*
- *¾ tsp garlic*
- *1 tsp green chilli paste*
- *½ tsp salt, or to taste*
- *¼ tsp turmeric*
- *¼ tsp granulated sugar*
- *1 tsp yogurt*
- *¼ tsp baking powder*
- *2 tbsp water*
- *Sunflower oil for shallow frying, approx. 50ml*

## METHOD

In a mixing bowl, combine all the listed ingredients with 2 tbsp water. It should form a nice malleable dough.

Form small 3cm long dumplings from the dough using the palms of your hands and forming a fist to create the muthia.

Shallow fry in a frying pan on medium heat. Partly cook them in the frying pan until they start to turn golden, at which point remove the muthia from the oil and transfer them to a heated wok on low heat and cook them for a further 20-25 minutes turning often until they are brown and crisp on all sides.

Simply serve with a cup of masala chai *(page 215)*

SPRING ONION DHEBRA - SAVOURY PANCAKES

# SPRING ONION DHEBRA (SAVOURY PANCAKES)

Every cuisine has their version of pancakes. This is the Indian savoury version. This is a recipe you can prepare in advance by making the batter and keeping in the fridge for a quick meal. They are pleasingly aromatic paired well with pickles and chutneys. I make a less spicy version for my kids who absolutely love these!

**SERVES 4**

## INGREDIENTS

- *175g juwar flour (Sorghun flour)*
- *85g chapati flour*
- *1 tsp ginger paste*
- *1 tsp green chilli paste*
- *1 tsp salt, or to taste*
- *¼ tsp turmeric*
- *1 tbsp yogurt*
- *2 tbsp sunflower oil, plus extra for cooking the dhebra*
- *5 tbsp spring onions, finely chopped*
- *175ml water*

## METHOD

In a large mixing bowl, combine all of the listed ingredients and mix well. The batter should be flowy but not runny. Allow the batter to rest for 30 minutes at room temperature.

Heat a tava or non-stick frying pan on medium-low heat. Add approx. half a teaspoon of oil to the tava/pan and swirl around to grease the base of the pan. Pour a ladle of the dhebra batter in the pan and spread evenly in circular moves using the base of the ladle. Add a few drops of oil around the sides and cook. When you see the dhebra edges start to crisp up, flip using a flat spatula and cook the other side for a further minute or so. Once it's nicely cooked, remove from the pan and repeat the process for the remaining batter. You don't need to cook all the batter. You can store in the fridge for up to 3 days, cook as and when required. Make sure to remove from the fridge at least half an hour before cooking and give it a good mix.

Serve with your favourite Indian pickle.

# KADHI (A TEMPERED SOUPY YOGURT)

A traditional sweet-sour-spicy yogurt soup thickened with chickpea flour and tempered with spices then simmered. This is super quick and delicious poured over khichdi. A simple recipe with simple ingredients and lots of flavours. A weekly staple in my house growing up. Perfect for the whole family. This also keeps well in the fridge for up to 2 weeks!

**SERVES 2**

## INGREDIENTS

### Ingredients for the khadi

- *Half handful of pigeon peas (Toovar lilva peas)*
- *4-5 fresh curry leaves*
- *1 tsp salt, or to taste*
- *¼ onion*
- *1 tsp cumin seeds*
- *1 inch piece of ginger*
- *1 green chilli*
- *1 tsp granulated sugar*
- *300g set yogurt*
- *450ml water*
- *¾ tbsp gram flour*
- *Chopped fresh coriander for garnish*

### Ingredients for Tempering

- *1 tbsp sunflower oil*
- *3 cloves*
- *¼ tsp asafoetida*
- *3-4 fenugreek seeds*
- *2 dried Kashmiri red chillies*
- *½ tsp black mustard seeds*
- *½ tsp cumin seeds*
- *8-10 fresh curry leaves*
- *1/8 tsp turmeric*

## METHOD

First let's make the masala paste for the kadhi. In a blender add the pigeon peas, onion, salt, curry leaves, cumin seeds, ginger and green chilli. Blend all together to a smooth paste.

In a jug add the set yogurt, water and gram flour. Whisk until there are no lumps of the gram flour. Now add the kadhi paste and whisk together vigorously until you create some foam on the surface of the mixture. Now add the granulated sugar, mix and set to one side.

In a saucepan, heat the sunflower oil, add mustard seed and let them crackle on a medium heat. As they start to crackle turn down the heat and add the remaining tempering spices. Fry on a low heat for about half a minute, then add the yogurt mixture slowly and carefully as it may splutter. Stir and mix well to combine. On a medium-low heat let the kadhi simmer for 10 minutes and serve.

# COURGETTE BAKRO

This is baked differently to the Vegetable bakro. This bakro is cooked on the stove in a frying pan. It's a humble dish that makes a great starter or snack. Great if you have a courgette lying around.

**SERVES 4**

## INGREDIENTS

- *2 courgettes, grated with a cheese grater*
- *200g fine white semolina*
- *¾ tsp ginger paste*
- *¾ tsp green chilli paste*
- *½ tsp salt*
- *¼ tsp turmeric*
- *1 ½ tbsp sunflower oil*
- *1 tbsp yogurt*
- *¼ tsp Eno/fruit salt*
- *280ml of water*

## METHOD

Take a small non-stick frying pan (not too wide as you want some thickness to your bakro) and place on a low heat with 1 tbsp of oil. Swirl the oil around the pan to grease the area.

Now in a large mixing bowl add all the ingredients listed (apart from the water) and whisk gently. Now add the water and whisk vigorously until fully combined. The mixture shouldn't be watery or drippy. A gloopy consistency is what you're looking for. Now pour this mix into the hot frying pan. It should sizzle. Evenly distribute the mixture across the pan. Cover with a lid and cook on a low heat for around 20 minutes until you start to see the edges browning. Then you need a bit of skill for the next bit. You need to flip the bakro like you would a pancake to cook on the other side. It does take some practice because the bakro is much thicker and heavier than flipping a pancake. Alternatively, you can use a large flat spatula to help you lift and flip the bakro. Once you have turned it over you will see the cooked side is golden brown and crispy. Cook for a further 20 minutes with the lid on. If you lift the bakro slightly with a spatula you should see it's cooked at crispy on the bottom too. If not, then cook for a little longer until it's golden brown.

Take off the heat, remove the lid from the pan and let it rest for 10 minutes. Place a serving plate on top of the frying pan and flip over with the pan so the bakro gently falls onto the plate.

You will have a beautiful golden coloured, crispy savoury cake. Cut into equal wedges like you would a cake and serve with a garlic and coriander chutney and a salad of your choice.

# CHILLI PANEER

Do you ever fancy a vegetarian dish, but the other half wants a meat dish? That's generally the case in my household! The sweetness of the onions and peppers fused with the spices and sauces will get you into a midweek sizzle! Once the base sauce is ready it's literally a case of deciding whether to throw in some chicken, or treat yourself to paneer or even Tofu! This dish is so versatile and trust me when I say this dish leaves you in no dilemmas!

**SERVES 2**

## INGREDIENTS

### For the paneer marinade

- *200g paneer/tofu diced into inch square cubes (or 3 chicken breasts cut into inch sized chunks)*
- *50g cornflour*
- *2 tbsp plain flour*
- *½ tsp salt*
- *½ tsp red chilli powder*
- *½ tsp ground black pepper*
- *1 tsp garlic paste*
- *1 tsp ginger paste*
- *50ml water*
- *Sunflower oil for deep frying*

### For the stir fry sauce

- *2 tbsp oil*
- *3 finely chopped cloves of garlic*
- *1 ½ inch finely chopped ginger*
- *1 large red onion chopped into large chunks*
- *½ green pepper medium sized diced*
- *½ red pepper medium sized diced*
- *4 spring onions finely sliced (leave around 1 tbsp of these to one side for garnish)*
- *2 fresh green chillies finely sliced*
- *2 tbsp white vinegar*
- *2 tbsp light soy sauce*
- *1 tbsp chilli sauce*
- *2 tbsp tomato ketchup*
- *½ tsp red chilli powder*
- *Cornflour slurry made from 1 tbsp cornflour and 4 tbsp water*
- *Chopped fresh coriander for garnish*

## METHOD

In a large mixing bowl, add the cornflour and plain flour. Also add the ginger and garlic pastes, black pepper, red chilli powder and salt. Mix well with the flours. Now add the water. whisk until you get a pancake like batter that's smooth and lump free. Now add the paneer (or tofu/chicken). Cover and marinate for 10-15 mins. Whilst this is marinating you can heat the oil for deep frying on a medium heat and start to prepare the veggies for the stir fry.

Uncover the marinated paneer mix again. Ensuring each piece is covered in batter, place into the hot oil carefully one by one and deep fry until the paneer or chicken pieces turn golden brown and crisp. Drain on tissue paper and set to one side.

Now, in a large wok, heat 2 tbsp of oil on a medium to low heat and sauté the chopped ginger and garlic. Add the sliced chillies, red onion, green and red peppers. Sauté for a minute or so on medium to high heat. Now add the spring onions (don't forget to leave 1 tbsp for garnishing at the end). Stir through with the rest of the veggies. Reduce to a medium heat and add the sauces and the spices – soy sauce, vinegar, chilli sauce, tomato ketchup and chilli powder. Mix everything together well and stir fry for a few minutes to let all the flavours infuse together. Now pour the cornflour slurry into the wok, continue to stir until the sauce thickens and has a glossy sheen to it. Turn the heat down low and add the fried paneer pieces. Put the lid on the pan and cook for a further 5 minutes stirring between. Finally, serve and garnish with spring onions and fresh coriander. Tastes delicious on its own or with rice.

# SOOJI DHOKLA

These Dhoklas are steamed, soft and fluffy savoury cakes made from rava (semolina). These are different to the usual Kamarn Dhoklas you may have eaten, which requires fermentation overnight. This Sooji Dhokla recipe is something my mum taught me as I was always stuck for quick snacks to feed unexpected guests. This is an instant tasty recipe that also goes well with a cup of tea. You can literally have these ready in under 30 minutes.

**MAKES 2 X 8 INCH ROUND TINS**
**SERVES 4**

## INGREDIENTS

### Ingredients for the Dhokla

- *300g coarse yellow semolina/rava*
- *3 tbsp chickpea flour*
- *1 tsp ginger paste*
- *1 tsp salt*
- *1 tbsp green chilli paste*
- *1 ½ tbsp yogurt*
- *3 tbsp sunflower oil*
- *200ml water*
- *¾ tsp of Eno (fruit salt) x 2 (one for each plate of dhokla)*
- *1 tbsp boiling water*
- *Red chilli powder for garnish*
- *Chopped fresh coriander for garnish*
- *Freshly grated coconut for garnish (optional)*

### Ingredients for Tempering

- *2 tbsp sunflower oil*
- *½ tsp mustard seeds*
- *1 tsp sesame seeds*

## METHOD

In a steamer add water and bring to boil. Whilst that's happening, in a mixing bowl mix all the ingredients together for the dhokla, except for the red chilli powder, fresh coriander and optional coconut. The batter should not be thick and gloopy, nor too runny. It should be a nice in between consistency. Now grease the pan/baking tin with oil. Add the Eno (fruit salt) to the batter pour over 1 tbsp hot boiling water and whisk in one direction and pour the batter into the greased tin. Spread evenly and shake the tin to even out the batter. Lightly sprinkle the top of the batter with some red chilli powder. Place the tin gently into the steamer, cover and steam for approx. 15-20 minutes. You can use an electric steamer if you wish. After 15 minutes or so lift the lid and check the dhokla has cooked through with a toothpick. It should come out clean. If so, the dhokla cake is ready. Remove the tin from the steamer and allow to cool for 5 minutes. Once it's slightly cooled, transfer to a chopping board and slice into diamond/ square shapes and place in a serving dish.

Now for tempering. Heat the oil in a small pan on a high flame and add the mustard seeds. Put the lid on the pan to avoid backsplash. Once you can hear mustard seeds start to pop reduce the heat to low, lift the lid slightly, add sesame seeds. Turn off the heat and pour the tempered spices evenly over the dhokla. Garnish with fresh coriander, and if you really want to show off to your guests then grate over some fresh coconut too. These dhoklas can be served warm or cool with some garlic and coriander chutney.

EGG
BHURJI

# EGG BHURJI

Breakfast, brunch or snack. This versatile recipe is quick to whip up any time of the day. The fragranced ingredients of this dish gives scrambled eggs a whole new meaning and a wonderful flavour in a matter of minutes. All the spices really awaken your taste buds. If you're having this substantial and satisfying meal for breakfast, it will set you up for the day!

**SERVES 2**

## INGREDIENTS

- *4 large free-range eggs*
- *4 slices of lightly toasted sourdough*
- *1 finely chopped onion*
- *1 finely chopped tomato*
- *Half green pepper finely diced*
- *½ tsp red chilli powder*
- *2 finely sliced green chillies*
- *1 tsp ginger paste*
- *1 tsp garlic paste*
- *½ tsp salt, or to taste*
- *½ tsp turmeric*
- *1 tbsp sunflower oil*
- *1 tsp butter*
- *Chopped fresh coriander for garnish*

## METHOD

In a non-stick frying pan, heat the oil over a medium heat. Add the onions and cook until translucent. Add the diced green peppers and cook for a further minute. Add the tomatoes and cook until the excess moisture has evaporated. Now you can add the ginger and garlic pastes, red chilli powder and turmeric. Stir well and cook for another minute or so, until the oil separates from the onion and tomato mixture. Now add the sliced green chillies and salt and stir well. Turn the heat down to low, add the eggs. Fold the eggs gently into the mixture until you start to see the eggs clumping up. Now turn the heat back up and stir the mixtures, breaking up the clumps of egg into smaller clumps. Once you see it all starting to come together, add the butter and stir until melted. Add the chopped coriander, stir and turn off the heat.

Serve on top on lightly toasted sourdough bread.

# PANEER STIR-FRY KATI ROLL

The ultimate veggie kebab! A spin on Indian fusion also known as Indochinese. The smooth texture from the paneer laced with the crunch of the stir-fried vegetables all rolled up in a softly flavoured cumin chapati will ignite satisfaction right to your core! It most definitely will sway those meat lovers in your household! A super quick weekday meal wrapped in a turmeric-ajwain chapati.

**SERVES 2**

## INGREDIENTS

- *200g of Paneer diced into 1cm cubes (soak in boiling water for 5 min to soften the paneer then drain)*
- *2 tbsp vegetable oil*
- *1 thinly sliced red onion*
- *1 tomato diced*
- *½ tsp tomato puree*
- *½ red pepper thinly sliced*
- *½ green pepper thinly sliced*
- *3 garlic cloves finely chopped*
- *1 inch ginger finely chopped*
- *1 tsp cumin seeds*
- *½ tsp turmeric*
- *1 tsp red chilli powder*
- *½ tsp coriander powder*
- *½ tsp salt, or to taste*
- *A squeeze of fresh lemon juice*
- *Chopped fresh coriander for garnish*
- *Darna Lasarn Chutney (recipe on page 189)*

### Ingredients for Turmeric and Cumin Chapati (makes 6)

- *200g Chapati flour (I suggest medium wholewheat chapati flour) + extra for dusting*
- *2 tbsp Sunflower oil*
- *½ tsp Turmeric*
- *½ tsp salt*
- *1 tsp Cumin seeds*
- *120ml boiling water*

## METHOD

Heat the oil in a wok on a high heat. Add the cumin seeds and stir for about 15-20 seconds until they release an aroma. Reduce the heat to a medium flame and add the onions. Fry until they become translucent. Add the diced garlic and ginger, and the tomato puree. Mix well. Add the turmeric, red chilli powder, coriander powder and salt. Now add the sliced peppers, diced tomatoes and mix well. Fry for a further 3-4 minutes until the peppers start to soften. Now add the paneer and stir well coating the paneer in all the spices. Squeeze in some fresh lemon juice and garnish with coriander. Set aside whilst you prepare the Turmeric and Cumin Chapati's.

Prepare the dough by adding sunflower oil to the chapati flour in a mixing bowl. Rub the oil into the flour using your finger tips. Now add the turmeric, salt and cumin seeds. Mix well into the flour. Make a well in the middle and add 120ml of boiling water, either boiled in a pan or in the kettle. Use a spoon at this point to initially combine the water into the flour mixture as it will be too hot to touch. After a minute or so you should be able to use your hands to start kneading the dough for 2-3 minutes until you have a soft and smooth dough ball.

Now divide the dough into 6 equal little dough balls. Take a piece of dough and roll it between your palms and flatten it slightly. Dip each side into the chapati flour. Now begin rolling your dough in a circular motion. Create an even surfaced, perfectly round chapati approx. 8 inches in diameter.

Preheat your tawa over a medium to low heat for 5 minutes. Place the rolled out chapati onto the tawa and cook for approx 10-15 seconds until little bubbles appear on the surface then flip it. Cook for a further 30 seconds. If you lift the chapati you will see the underside has little brown spots all over. At this point flip it again and cook for 10-15 seconds more until more darker spots appear. This is the stage where the chapati should rise. Don't worry if they don't rise initially. It will come with practice. Flip the chapati one last time and place on this side up on kitchen tissue. I don't normally butter these chapatis for the kati roll, but you can if your tastebuds prefer.

Repeat this process for the remaining dough balls.

Now for the most exciting part, take a freshly cooked cumin chapati, place 2-3 tbsp of the paneer stir fry vertically in the centre of the chapati and then roll it up. Dip into some Darna Lasarn Chutney. It's so delicious, you won't be able to get enough.

# MASALA EGGS

We always have eggs in our house as it's such a versatile ingredient. There are a variety of things you can whip up with the humble egg. My masala eggs are a quick lunchtime spice craving either on their own, with a dollop of ketchup, or in a sandwich.

**SERVES 2**

## INGREDIENTS

- *4 hardboiled eggs, halved*
- *2 tsp sunflower oil*
- *1 tsp whole cumin seeds*
- *½ finely chopped onion*
- *1 tsp tomato puree*
- *½ tsp garlic paste*
- *½ tsp ginger paste*
- *¼ tsp turmeric*
- *1 tsp red chilli powder*
- *½ tsp coriander powder*
- *2 tbsp Greek yogurt*
- *Chopped fresh coriander for garnish*
- *½ tsp salt, or to taste*

## METHOD

Heat a frying pan on low to medium heat with the oil, add the cumin seeds and cook until fragrant. Add the onion and fry until slightly browned. Add the tomato puree and stir well. Add the ginger and garlic pastes, red chilli powder, turmeric, coriander powder and salt. Mix well to create a thick paste with the onions and tomato puree. Cook for 3-4 minutes until you start to see the oil coming away at the edges from the paste. Now add the eggs and mix well covering the eggs evenly with the mixture. Turn the heat down to low and cook for a further 3-4 minutes. Add the Greek yogurt and cook for a further minute. Add chopped coriander to garnish.

Why not have an egg butty. Put the masala eggs into a soft bread roll and enjoy! I want to say put the eggs in a BARM because I'm from Lancashire, but for argument's sake I'll say a 'bread roll'.

# BAKRO (VEGETABLE BAKE)

This can be such a versatile recipe that you can make out of any vegetable! Whatever veggies you have left in the bottom of your fridge. It can be anything from cabbage, spinach, peas or peppers. You could even put some grated cheese in there! Throw whatever tickles your fancies into a bakro and you've got yourself a banger!

**SERVES 4**

## INGREDIENTS

- *400g fine semolina*
- *2 medium grated carrots*
- *½ red onion, chopped*
- *½ white onion, chopped*
- *75g of garden peas (tinned, frozen or fresh)*
- *75g sweetcorn (tinned, frozen or fresh)*
- *1 tsp salt*
- *¼ tsp turmeric*
- *1 ½ tsp ginger paste*
- *½ tsp green chilli paste*
- *3 tbsp oil*
- *1 ½ tbsp yogurt*
- *280ml water*
- *½ tsp Eno/fruit salt*

### Ingredients for the tempering

- *2 tbsp sunflower oil*
- *1 tsp mustards seeds*
- *8-10 curry leaves*
- *1 tsp sesame seeds*

## METHOD

Mix all the ingredients, apart from the Eno/bicarb, together in a large mixing bowl. Add half a pint of water and stir together well. the mixtures shouldn't be too runny. A gloopy texture that falls off the spoon like 'plop'. You don't want it dripping off the spoon.

This can be kept in the fridge until you're ready to cook.

Pre-heat the oven to gas mark 6/200 degrees/180 degrees for fan oven.

Add the Eno to the bakro mix and stir well. Pour the mixture into a pre-greased square baking tin and bake in the oven for 30-40 minutes. Make sure it's cooked in the middle before removing from the oven. Do the cake test, where you insert a thin skewer/toothpick into the middle of the cake, it should come out clean with no streaks of batter.

Remove from the oven and prepare the tempering. In a small saucepan, heat the oil on a high heat and add the mustard seeds and put the lid on the pan. As they start to pop, reduce the heat to low and throw in the curry leaves. Give the pan a swirl and add the sesame seeds. Take off the heat and pour the tempered spices over the bakro.

You serve this as an appetiser cut in small bitesize pieces, or cut into individual square portions for a meal.

CREAMY MATAR PANEER

# CREAMY MATAR PANEER

A restaurant style creamy, delicious and rich paneer curry with peas. A curry base made of mushed onions, tomato puree, ginger, garlic, red chilli powder, curry paste, kasuri methi and a large tub of cream. This dish goes well with paratha or naan and jeera rice. Vegans can substitute the paneer with tofu and still enjoy the deliciousness.

**SERVES 4**

## INGREDIENTS

- *200g paneer*
- *2 onions, blended to a mush*
- *2 handfulls of petit pois*
- *100g of tomato puree*
- *1 tsp ginger paste*
- *1 ½ tsp garlic paste*
- *1 tsp dry coriander powder*
- *1 tsp red chilli powder*
- *¾ tsp turmeric*
- *1/8 tsp asafoetida*
- *1 tbsp madras paste*
- *2 tbsp fresh fenugreek leaves (methi), finely chopped*
- *600ml Single cream*
- *1 tsp salt, or to taste*
- *4 tbsp sunflower oil, plus extra for shallow frying the paneer.*

## METHOD

Dice the paneer into 1-2cm pieces. Soak in lukewarm water for 10 minutes. This softens the paneer so it's not as dense. Drain and pat dry with kitchen paper. Shallow fry on a medium heat until lightly golden on all sides. Drain on some kitchen paper and keep to one side whilst you prepare the sauce.

In a large wide saucepan, heat 4 tbsp sunflower oil on a medium heat and add the asafoetida. Turn the heat down to very low and carefully add the mushed onions, avoiding any spitting from oil. Lightly brown the onions until they are golden. Now add the tomato puree, mix well with the cooked onions. Sauté for a few minutes before adding the ginger and garlic pastes, madras paste, dry coriander powder, red chilli powder, turmeric and salt. Mix everything together well and cook for 5 minutes, until you can see the oil separating at the edges. Now add the fried paneer and the petit pois and mix well. Keeping the heat on low, add the single cream, stir well and simmer for 5 minutes stirring often to prevent the cream from splitting. Add a final flourish of the fresh fenugreek leaves and take off the heat.

Serve with jeera rice and naan.

# VEGAN

GUJARATI KANDA BATETA

# GUJARATI KANDA BATETA

A classic Gujarati dish that is made with the humblest of ingredients. A potato and onion stir fry which doesn't have any garlic or ginger. Nevertheless, trust me when I say it's full of flavour. Made from ingredients which are readily available in your kitchen. Even if you are left with nothing but onions and potatoes then this is the dish for you.

**SERVES 2**

## INGREDIENTS

- *3 medium king Edward potatoes*
- *4 medium white/red onions (tastes great with either)*
- *½ tsp black mustard seeds*
- *½ tsp whole cumin seeds*
- *3 tbsp sunflower oil*
- *½ tsp turmeric*
- *1 tsp red chilli powder*
- *¾ tsp dry coriander powder*
- *¾ tsp salt, or to taste*
- *Freshly chopped coriander for garnish*

## METHOD

Firstly, prepare the potatoes and onions.

Quarter the potatoes along the longest length. Then thinly slice each quarter into triangular shapes (0.5cm thickness). Place the chopped potatoes into a mixing bowl.

Now, peel the onions, cut in half and finely slice them. Add these to a separate mixing bowl.

Take a frying pan and place on medium-high heat. Add the sunflower oil, black mustard seeds and cumin seeds. As the seeds start to pop, turn the heat down to low and add the turmeric. Swirl around with the tempered spices.

Now add the chopped potatoes and stir. Add the dry coriander powder and mix again.

Continue to cook the potatoes on a low heat for 5 minutes with the lid on before adding the sliced onions. Stir everything together gently and cook for approx. 20-25 minutes without the lid until the potatoes are cooked and the onions have softened. Now add the red chilli powder and salt. Stir through gently. Garnish with coriander and serve with Bakri.

SHALLOT RAVAIYA

# SHALLOT RAVAIYA

The humble shallot can be turned into something so beautiful with this dish. The nutty gravy is just divine and when scooped up with fresh chapatis it will definitely tickle your tastebuds. Serve with a glass of Chaas for the ultimate combo. This dish brings back many happy childhood memories.

**SERVES 2**

## INGREDIENTS

- *400g shallots*
- *3 tbsp dry coriander*
- *4 tbsp coarsely ground plain unsalted peanuts*
- *1 tsp red chilli powder*
- *1 tsp salt, or to taste*
- *1 tsp garlic paste*
- *½ tsp turmeric*
- *Pinch of asafoetida*
- *Pinch of bicarbonate soda*
- *½ tsp granulated sugar*
- *3 tbsp sunflower oil*
- *100ml warm water*
- *2 tbsp coriander, finely chopped (plus extra for garnish)*
- *1 tbsp freshly chopped green garlic (optional)*

## METHOD

Peel the shallots and create 2 slits in each of the shallots, creating a crosscut. Make the slits as deep as ¾ of the way down the shallot. Set aside while you prepare the masala stuffing.

In a mixing bowl, add the dry coriander, coarsely ground peanuts, chilli powder, salt, garlic paste, turmeric, asafoetida, bicarbonate soda, granulated sugar, oil and finely chopped coriander. Combine everything with your fingers.

Now carefully stuff the prepared shallots with the masala stuffing.

Carefully place each of the stuffed shallots in a heavy bottom saucepan. Add 100ml warm water.

Place the pan on a low heat for 30 minutes. Occasionally, carefully move the shallots around the pan using the back of a spoon. Do not mix or stir as this will break up the shallots.

After 30 minutes the shallots should be soft and cooked through.

Garnish with finely chopped coriander, and fresh green garlic (optional).

Serve with Bakri, Toor Dal Khichdi and Chaas.

# VEGETABLE MANCHURIAN

This labour of love can be one of the most addictive Indochinese dishes. Dumpling made from finely chopped veggies dunked into a sauce that explodes with hot, sweet, sour and salty flavours. It has a glossy, rich sauce that is impossible to resist. Even tastes great as a veggie option to spaghetti and meatballs.

**SERVES 4**

## INGREDIENTS

### Ingredients for the koftas

- *Half of a white cabbage, finely chopped*
- *Half of a cauliflower, finely chopped*
- *2 medium carrots, finely chopped*
- *2 spring onions, finely chopped*
- *1 large red pepper, finely chopped*
- *4 tbsp cornflour*
- *2 tbsp plain flour*
- *1 tbsp grated ginger*
- *1 tbsp grated garlic*
- *½ tsp green chilli paste*
- *½ tsp salt*
- *½ tsp ground black pepper*
- *Sunflower oil for deep frying*

### Ingredients for The Gravy

- *2 tbsp sunflower oil*
- *10-12 cloves of garlic, finely chopped*
- *3 tbsp grated ginger*
- *1 red onion, chopped*
- *4 green chillies, finely chopped*
- *3 tbsp soy sauce*
- *2 tbsp garlic chilli sauce*
- *½ tsp granulated sugar*
- *400ml water*
- *2 tbsp cornflour + 4 tbsp water*
- *1 tsp course black pepper*
- *2 spring onions, finely chopped for garnish*
- *Freshly chopped coriander for garnish*

## METHOD

Firstly, to make the koftas, all the veg needs to be finely chopped. You can do this in a food processor if you have one. Alternatively. you could grate the veggies.

In a large mixing bowl add the finely chopped cabbage, cauliflower, carrots, red pepper and spring onions. To this add the cornflour, plain flour, grated ginger and garlic, green chilli paste, salt and pepper. Using your hands, mix and combine all the ingredients together. The veggies will release their own natural juices to help bind everything together to form a slight dough like consistency. Allow the mixture to rest.

Meanwhile heat the sunflower oil in a large wok/karai on medium heat (175 degrees) for deep frying. . Once the oil is ready you prepare your kofta balls with the vegetable mixture you made. Take approx. 1 tbsp of the mixture and roll into little kofta balls using the palms of your hands. Add to the oil and fry until golden brown. Repeat for the remaining mixture. Cook in small batches of 3-4 koftas at a time. Once fried transfer the koftas to a dish lined with kitchen paper to drain the excess oil. Once all your koftas are fried set them to one side.

Now you can prepare the Manchurian sauce.

Heat a large wok on high heat. Add the sunflower oil and the chopped garlic and grated ginger. Toss around in the oil and sauté for 10-15 seconds. Add the chopped red onion and green chillies and fry for a further 30 seconds. Add the soy sauce, garlic chilli sauce, coarse black pepper and granulated sugar. Mix well. Now add the water and bring to boil stirring continuously. Now reduce the heat to low.

In a small bowl mix the 2 tbsp cornflour with 4 tbsp water to make a cornflour slurry. Add this mix to the wok. Mix well until the sauce thickens and continue to cook on a low heat for 5 minutes, stirring often.

Now add the fried kofta balls to the wok and gently mix with the gravy. Simmer for 3-4 minutes to allow the flavours of the gravy to cover the surface of the koftas. Garnish with freshly chopped spring onions and coriander.

This dish can be enjoyed on its own or topped on noodles/spaghetti.

# GUJARATI BHEGA DAL BHAT (DHANSAK)

This is a warming hearty stew like dish packed with tangy, sweet and spicy flavours. A classic Indian food recipe that combines dal and rice with all the goodness of the veggies. This can be a real heart-warming meal on those breezy evenings.

**SERVES 4**

## INGREDIENTS

### Ingredients for the dal

- *100g tuvar dal*
- *1 tomato, roughly chopped*
- *1 tsp oil*
- *Pinch of salt*
- *500ml water*

### Other ingredients

- *200g long grain basmati rice*
- *600ml hot water*
- *3 tbsp sunflower oil*
- *2-3 cloves*
- *½ tsp black mustard seeds*
- *½ tsp cumin seeds*
- *1/8 tsp asafoetida*
- *1 small aubergine, diced into cm cubes*
- *1 medium potato, diced into cm cubes*
- *¼ onion, finely chopped*
- *50g pigeon peas*
- *10-12 tindora (ivy gourd) each one sliced lengthways into 8 equal pieces*
- *50g guvar (cluster beans)*
- *2 tsp salt, or to taste*
- *2 tsp ginger paste*
- *1 ¼ tsp green chilli paste*
- *Juice of ¼ lemon*
- *½ tsp turmeric*
- *2 tsp granulated sugar*
- *¼ tsp garam masala*
- *Freshly chopped coriander for garnish*

## METHOD

Wash the basmati rice and soak in lukewarm water whilst you do the initial cooking process.

Wash the tuvar dal and transfer to a pressure cooker along with the chopped tomato, sunflower oil and a pinch of salt. Pour in 500mls of hot water. Pressure cook for 15-20 mins until cooked through. Let it cool slightly before blending to a liquid. I normally use a hand blender for this, but you can use any blender. Set to one side.

In a large saucepan on medium heat, add 3 tbsp sunflower oil, cloves, black mustard seeds and cumin seeds. Wait till the mustard seeds start to pop and sizzle before adding the asafoetida. Now add the chopped veggies (aubergine, potato, onion, pigeon peas, tindora and guwar). Mix well with the tempered spices and cook for 10 minutes, stirring often.

Now add the ginger paste, chilli paste, salt, lemon, turmeric and sugar. Mix well with all the veggies.

Now add the liquidised tuvar dal to the saucepan. Combine well with all the other ingredients. Add the garam masala, stir and cook for 5 minutes on a low heat.

Finally, add the soaked rice along with 600ml of hot water. Gently stir everything together, careful not to break the rice. Cover the pan and simmer on a low heat until the rice is cooked through. It should have a thick soupy consistency, so add water during the cooking process if you feel it is necessary.

Once cooked, garnish with freshly chopped coriander and serve while it's warm. Perfect for a warm winter's evening!

# CUTLETS

These are basically mini veggie patties, but oh so yummy. They are made using a combination of veggies with potatoes for binding. They are coated in semolina then pan fried to create a crisp outer texture.

**SERVES 2-3**

## INGREDIENTS

### Ingredients for the veggie filling

- *3 medium potatoes, boiled/pressure cooked with skin on*
- *2 slices of stale bread, blitzed to breadcrumbs*
- *1 small red onion, finely diced*
- *1 small carrot, peeled and finely chopped*
- *1 red pepper, finely chopped*
- *½ tsp garlic paste*
- *½ tsp ginger paste*
- *1 tsp green chilli paste*
- *Handful of garden peas*
- *2 tbsp freshly chopped coriander*
- *½ tsp salt, or to taste*

### Ingredients for the coating

- *3 tbsp coarse semolina*
- *3 tbsp readymade breadcrumbs*
- *Sunflower oil for deep frying*

## METHOD

Peel the skin from the cooked potatoes and mash in a mixing bowl. Add the rest of the ingredients listed for the veggie filling. Mix and combine well.

In a saucer/small dish, combine the ingredients for the coating – coarse semolina and breadcrumbs. Set to the side for later.

Oil a surface well and flatten the veggie filling using your hands. Flatten to a thickness of around 2cm. Using a 5cm cookie cutter, cut out shapes of the veggie filling to form cutlets.

Dip each cutlet into the coating mixture. Evenly coat each side ensuring full coverage. Repeat for each cutlet.

Heat sunflower oil to 180 degrees on medium heat for deep frying.

Deep fry each cutlet, and using a slotted spoon turn gently in the oil to cook both sides evenly. Fry until they are golden brown on both sides. Once cooked transfer to kitchen paper.

Serve the cutlets warm with a red chilli sauce. Enjoy either on their own or in a sandwich.

# TOMATO MIXED DAL

This is a healthy yet aromatic and hearty dish that is great for those busy days! Dal is a staple in every Indian home and there are many variations. This is a mild, slightly tangy and comforting dal that goes perfectly with chapatis.

**SERVES 2**

## INGREDIENTS

- *25g split chana dal*
- *25g toor dal*
- *25g masoor dal*
- *25g urad dal*
- *1 tbsp sunflower oil*
- *3-4 curry leaves*
- *1/8 tsp asafoetida*
- *1 medium onion, blended to a puree*
- *200g tinned chopped tomatoes*
- *½ tsp garlic paste*
- *½ tsp ginger paste*
- *1 tsp red chilli powder*
- *½ tsp cumin seeds*
- *½ tsp cumin powder*
- *½ tsp coriander powder*
- *½ tsp turmeric*
- *½ tsp garam masala*
- *½ tsp salt, or to taste*
- *Chopped fresh coriander for garnish*

## METHOD

Pressure cook the lentils for 2 whistles/15 mins in 1 litre of warm water. Let the pressure cooker cool before removing the lid. Don't worry if the lentils aren't fully cooked.

In a large saucepan, heat the sunflower oil on medium heat, add the cumin seeds. As they start to sizzle and brown, reduce the heat to low and add the curry leaves. Now add the asafoetida and swirl around in the oil. Add the pureed onion and sauté on a low heat until they just start to brown. Now add the tinned chopped tomatoes and mix well with the onions. Cook for 5 minutes then add the ginger and garlic pastes, cumin powder, coriander powder, turmeric, garam masala and salt. Sauté the spices in the onion and tomato mix for 5 minutes before adding the cooked lentils along with the water left in the pressure cooker. Combine all the ingredients well together with the lentils. Continue to simmer and stir often on a low heat until the lentils are cooked (test the lentils with the back of a spoon against the side of the pan). Once cooked, garnish with freshly chopped coriander and serve with warm chapatis.

VAGHARELI MAKAI

# VAGHARELI MAKAI

A spiced sweetcorn stir fry. Fresh and packed full of flavour. The easiest of all healthy lunchtime meals. You can whip up this scrumptious sweetcorn stir fry in minutes. The corn marries beautifully with the crunchy peanuts, ginger and chillies. A few squeezes of lime brings the flavours alive!

**SERVES 4**

## INGREDIENTS

- *500g Frozen sweetcorn, pat dry on kitchen paper*
- *1 tsp garlic paste*
- *1 tsp green chilli paste*
- *1 tbsp coarsely crushed unsalted peanuts*
- *¼ tsp turmeric*
- *2 tbsp sunflower oil*
- *1/8 tsp asafoetida*
- *¼ tsp lemon juice*
- *½ tsp black mustard seeds*
- *½ tsp salt, or to taste*
- *Chopped fresh coriander for garnish*
- *Indian sev gathia (optional), readily available in most supermarkets and Indian food stores*

## METHOD

Heat sunflower oil in a wok on medium-high heat. Add the black mustard seeds. When they start to pop turn the heat down to low and add the asafoetida. Add the garlic paste, green chilli paste, peanuts, turmeric and salt. Continuously stir on a low heat for 30 seconds. Add the sweetcorn and mix well incorporating all the spices within. Cook for 15 minutes on medium heat, stirring occasionally. Add lemon juice and stir through.

Garnish with coriander and serve with a sprinkling of Indian sev gathia.

# UNDHIYU (MIXED VEGETABLE CURRY)

This is a vegetarian dish bursting with flavours, and is usually served at special occasions like weddings. I remember it being served at my own wedding. This is a labour of love with different elements but I promise it's worth every bite.

A recipe from my grandad that I will cherish forever. There was no one that could make Undhiyu like him. This is his exact recipe but it always tasted better when he made it. Now that he is no longer with us, this is the closest I can get to the taste of this delectable and luxurious dish.

**SERVES 4**

## INGREDIENTS

### Ingredients for the masala

- *1 tsp ginger paste*
- *1 ½ tsp garlic paste*
- *1 ½ tsp green chilli paste*
- *3 tbsp fresh coriander, finely chopped*
- *2 tsp dry coriander powder*
- *1 tbsp coarsely crushed unsalted peanuts*
- *1 tbsp freshly grated coconut*
- *1 tsp sesame seeds*
- *2 tbsp unsalted cashew nuts, split in half*
- *1 tbsp raisins*
- *½ tsp garam masala*
- *1 tsp lemon juice*
- *2 tsp granulated sugar*
- *½ tsp red chilli powder*
- *1 tsp salt, or to taste*
- *3-4 tbsp sunflower oil*

### Other Ingredients

- *¼ lb purple yam, peeled and cut into 2 inch pieces*
- *1 medium sized sweet potato, peeled and cut into 2 inch pieces*
- *2 medium white potatoes, peeled and cut into 2 inch pieces*
- *1 medium sized aubergine, cut into 6-8 equal sized chunks*
- *450g surti papdi lilva (flat green beans)*
- *1 ripe banana, keep the skin on, score the skin down the length to reveal the banana inside and cut into 2 inch chunks*
- *1 tsp ajwain seeds*
- *1/8 tsp asafoetida*
- *850ml warm water*
- *4 tbsp Sunflower oil, plus extra for deep frying*
- *Chopped fresh coriander and fresh green garlic for garnish*

### METHOD

Heat sunflower oil in a wok for deep frying. Heat on a medium heat to 180 degrees. Deep fry the chopped purple yam, sweet potato and white potato until they turn golden brown in colour. Drain on kitchen paper and set to one side.

Place a large deep saucepan on medium heat with 4 tbsp sunflower oil. Add the ajwain seeds and let them sizzle for a few seconds and then add the asafoetida. Swirl around in the oil, add the surti papdi lilva (flat green beans) and the chopped aubergine along with 850ml warm water. Simmer and cook on medium heat for 30 minutes, stirring occasionally.

Meanwhile prepare the masala from the listed ingredients for the masala. Set to one side.

After the 30 minutes have passed, add the fried vegetables along with the prepared masala mixture. Mix well combining all the vegetables well with the masala.

Continue to cook on medium heat for a further 20 minutes, stirring occasionally.

Now add the chopped banana and cook for another 10 minutes.

Finish with a garnish of freshly chopped green garlic and coriander.

Serve with puri for a rich and decadent vegetarian meal.

# VEGETABLE SOUP

This easy healthy delicious soup made with spices is the perfect hearty bowl of goodness you need when feeling low. My mum always brings me a pot of this when I'm feeling under the weather. A tasty pick me up.

**SERVES 2**

### INGREDIENTS

- *½ floret broccoli, cut to bitesize pieces*
- *¾ onion, roughly chopped*
- *2 carrots, sliced*
- *1 handful of garden peas*
- *½ medium potato, roughly chopped*
- *½ tsp garlic paste*
- *½ tsp crushed black pepper*
- *1 vegetable stock cube*
- *½ tsp butter*
- *¼ tsp green chilli paste*
- *¼ tsp salt*
- *570ml water*

### METHOD

Add all the ingredients to a pressure cooker. Cook for 3 whistles/20minutes. Once cooked, let the pressure cooker cool down naturally before removing the lid.

Blend ¾ of the cooked soup with a blender and leave the rest whole for texture.

Serve hot with buttered bread rolls.

BATETA VADA-PAV

# BATETA VADA-PAV

This is another taste tantalising street food of India. The dish consists of a deep fried potato dumpling (vada) placed inside a bread roll (pav) accompanied with a red chilli sauce, green chutney and tamarind chutney. One bite of this vada pav will be like an explosion of flavours in your mouth. This does require some prep work but believe me it will all seem worth it!

There was a shop around the corner from my grandparents in India that sold these. The memories still make my mouth water.

**SERVES 6**

## INGREDIENTS

### Ingredients for the stuffing

- *2 medium potatoes, boiled/pressure cooked, peeled and mashed*
- *1 tsp garlic paste*
- *2 green chillies, blended to paste*
- *¼ tsp salt, or to taste*
- *1 tbsp freshly chopped coriander*
- *¼ tsp turmeric*
- *1 tsp split yellow mung dal, roasted*
- *¼ tsp garam masala*
- *½ tsp lemon juice*

### Ingredients for the batter

- *175g chickpea flour*
- *¼ tsp salt, or to taste*
- *1 tbsp sunflower oil*
- *Water*

### Red chilli sauce

- *2 sweet ramiro peppers (sweet pointed red peppers)*
- *2 garlic cloves*
- *Juice of half lemon*
- *¼ tsp salt, or to taste*
- *1 tsp olive oil*

### Green Chutney

- *30g fresh coriander*
- *1 green chilli*
- *3 garlic cloves*
- *1/3 tsp sugar*
- *¼ tsp ground cumin powder*
- *¼ tsp salt, or to taste*
- *1 tbsp water*

### Tamarind Chutney

- *1 ½ tsp tamarind paste*
- *1 tbsp jaggery*
- *1 tbsp warm water*
- *¼ red chilli powder*
- *½ dry coriander powder*
- *¼ tsp salt, or to taste*

### Other ingredients

- *Sunflower oil for deep frying*
- *6 Mini white bread rolls*

## BATETA VADA-PAV

### METHOD

Combine all the ingredients listed for the stuffing. Mix well and divide into 6 equal sized balls. Place in the fridge for 30 minutes.

Start to prepare all the chutneys.

First for the red chilli sauce, blend the ramiro peppers with the garlic cloves, then add the lemon juice, salt and olive oil. Mix well and refrigerate until ready to eat.

For the green chutney, blend all the ingredients listed until you have a smooth chutney. Refrigerate until ready to eat.

Lastly, the tamarind chutney. In a small bowl mix together the warm water with the jaggery. This will help the jaggery break down into smaller grains. Mix together with the remaining ingredients listed until you have a smooth chutney. Refrigerate until ready to eat.

Prepare the batter by whisking together the chickpea flour with salt and oil. Add the water until you get a gloopy consistency. Whisk in one direction continuously until the batter comes together.

Heat sunflower oil in a wok/deep frying pan. Heat on medium heat to 180 degrees. When the oil is hot, add ½ tsp of the hot oil to the batter mix and stir well.

Now get the stuffing bateta balls. Take one of the bateta balls and dip into the chickpea flour batter. Gently coat the ball evenly to form a bateta vada. Place each bateta vada into the hot oil. Cook and turn the vadas with a slotted spoon and fry until they become lightly crisp and golden in colour. Place the cooked bateta vadas onto kitchen paper to drain any excess oil and continue to cook the remaining vadas by dipping each ball into the chickpea batter and gently frying.

Assembling the Vada Pav:

Slice the bread rolls (pav) without breaking them into halves. Spread the bottom half with the red chilli chutney, the top half with the green chutney and place the hot fried bateta vada inside the bread roll. Drizzle some tamarind chuntey over the bateta vada and sandwich together. Serve immediately.

# KHICHU

Steamed rice flour dumplings. So simple and easy to make with rice flour and a few spices. A healthy and tasty steamed dumpling recipe that I could eat any time of the day! It has a soft and smooth texture.

A perfect light lunch that is gluten free and vegan.

**SERVES 4**

## INGREDIENTS

- *300g rice flour*
- *600ml warm water*
- *2 tsp green chilli paste*
- *1 tsp cumin seeds*
- *¼ tsp bicarbonate soda*
- *1 handful tapioca pearls*
- *1 ¼ tsp salt, or to taste*
- *Sunflower oil for greasing*
- *Olive oil, red chilli powder and sesame seeds for garnishing.*

## METHOD

In a large saucepan, add the warm water, cumin seeds, salt, green chilli paste and bicarbonate soda. Stir together and place on a medium heat. Before you bring to boil add the tapioca pearls and bring to boil. Then add the rice flour. Using the long end of a wooden spoon, stir the mix vigorously on a high heat until it all starts come together.

Your khichu dough is now ready so take it off the heat.

Prepare to steam by filling the bottom of your steamer with water. Grease your steaming plate with oil and place in the steamer. Take a large serving spoon of the khichu dough, roll into a ball using the palms of your hands (grease your hands with oil if necessary). Flatten dough ball slightly with the palm of your hands and pierce a hole in the middle with your thumb to create a doughnut looking dumpling. Place into the steaming plate and repeat for the rest of the dough.

Steam the khichu on medium heat for 25 minutes precisely.

Serve hot with a drizzle of olive oil, a sprinkling of red chilli powder and sesame seeds.

Nothing else is required to accompany this dish, it's simply delicious eaten on its own.

# MIXED DAL PALAK

I love to add a twist to my dishes and this dal inspired recipe definitely has one! Spinach adds great value to a healthy lifestyle and chopping a good amount into dal not only adds flavour and texture but boosts those iron levels which will add a spring to your step! Almost like a soup keeping you warm on those cold winter nights. It's such a simple dish that requires minimum prep, but 100% satisfaction is guaranteed.

**SERVES 2**

## INGREDIENTS

- *200g Yellow split gram dal (yellow moong dal)*
- *150g Urad dal*
- *50g Chana dal*
- *1 tbsp Toor dal*
- *50g chopped spinach*
- *1 tbsp sunflower oil*
- *1 tsp black mustard seeds*
- *Pinch of asafoetida*
- *1 dried Kashmiri red chilli*
- *4-5 curry leaves*
- *¾ tsp turmeric*
- *1 tsp dry ground coriander*
- *½ tsp garlic paste*
- *½ tsp green chilli paste*
- *½ tsp salt, or to taste*
- *Chopped fresh coriander for garnish*

## METHOD

In a large mixing bowl mix all 4 of the different dals and soak in water for at least 2 hours. This helps to speed up the cooking time. You can by all means soak the dal in the morning to cook later in the evening.

In a large saucepan, heat the oil on a high heat, add mustard seeds and put a lid on the pan. When the mustard seeds start to pop turn the heat right down. Once the popping starts to slow down, add the asafoetida, dried Kashmiri red chilli and curry leaves. Let them sizzle for a few seconds. Drain the water from the dal. Carefully add a large spoonful of the dal to the saucepan and put the lid back on the pan. This will prevent the mustard seeds and oil spitting back at you. That initial spoonful of dal will have settled the oil in the saucepan, so you can lift the lid and add the remaining dal to the saucepan. Mix the dal with the tempered spices. Now you can add the turmeric, dry coriander, garlic and chilli paste and salt. Mix all the ingredients well on a low heat. Now add hot water to the pan and immerse the dal in enough water so it's around 2 inches above the level of the dal. Simmer on a low heat for around 20-25 minutes, stirring regularly to ensure the dal doesn't stick to the bottom of the pan. As the water bubbles away and starts to evaporate, you will see the dal turn to a thick soupy consistency. At this point check how much the dal is cooked by taking a small amount on your spoon and squishing some of the dal between your fingers. If it still feels a little hard, then it probably needs another 10 minutes or so to cook. You may need to add some more water at this stage to fully cook the dal. Put the lid on the dal and simmer for a further 10 minutes on a low heat. The consistency of the dal shouldn't be too thick or too thin. It's should have the consistency of porridge. Garnish with fresh coriander and serve with chapatis to scoop up all that soupy goodness.

# DAL VADA

Crunchy savoury deep fried spiced fritters that make a great tea time snack. These vada are crispy and addictive in taste! So addictive, you can't stop at one.

**SERVES 4**

### INGREDIENTS

- *200g chana dal (split chickpeas)*
- *3 tbsp urad dal (split black gram)*
- *3 dried Kashmiri red chillies*
- *1 onion, finely chopped*
- *2 green chillies, finely sliced*
- *1 ½ inch ginger, finely grated*
- *3 tbsp coriander, finely chopped*
- *¾ tsp salt, or to taste*
- *Sunflower oil, for deep frying*

### METHOD

In a large mixing bowl filled with water, soak the dals and dried Kashmiri chillies for 2-3 hours.

Drain out the water. Now blend the dals and chillies into a coarse mixture. No need to add any water as we want a thick gloopy batter.

Transfer the blended mix to a large mixing bowl to which, add the finely chopped onion, sliced green chillies, grated ginger, chopped coriander and salt. Mix all the ingredients together well.

Heat the sunflower oil in a wok on medium heat to 180 degrees. You can form the vada shapes while the oil heats up.

Start to form dal vadas rolling small balls of the batter, approx. 3cm in diameter (grease the palms of your hands if you find the batter is sticking). Ever so slightly flatten them with your palms keeping some depth to the vadas. Place each one on some grease proof paper. Once they are all rolled out you can start to fry them a few at a time. Don't overcrowd the frying pan. Fry them on both sides until golden brown. Drain on some kitchen paper. Serve with some chutney or raita. Which ever tickles your fancy.

# ONION PAKORAS

Onion fritters made with chickpea flour. A popular Indian street food. They are deep fried until crunchy and golden.

Serve as a snack or starter with your favourite chutney or raita.

**SERVES 2-4**

## INGREDIENTS

- *3 onions, finely sliced*
- *6 green chillies, finely sliced*
- *1 tbsp ginger, finely chopped*
- *2 tbsp fresh coriander, finely chopped*
- *1 tsp red chilli powder*
- *¼ tsp turmeric*
- *¼ tsp bicarbonate soda*
- *1/8 tsp asafoetida*
- *200g gram flour*
- *3 tbsp rice flour*
- *2 tbsp Sunflower oil, plus extra for deep frying.*
- *2 tbsp water*

## METHOD

In a large mixing bowl combine the finely sliced onions with the chopped ginger, green chillies, red chilli powder, turmeric, asafoetida, salt and chopped coriander. Let the spices infuse in the onions for 5 minutes.

Meanwhile start to heat the oil on medium heat for deep frying.

In the onion mix bowl add the remaining ingredients, gram flour, rice flour, oil and water. This is not a runny mixture at all, so you only need a couple of tablespoons of water. Mix well. Now add the bicarbonate soda and stir through.

Test the oil has reached the desired temperature by dropping a small amount of the pakora mixture into the pan. If it sinks to the bottom, the oil is not hot enough. If the batter rises to the top, then you're ready to fry. Keep the heat on medium heat.

Gently spoon in tablespoon size dollops of the pakora mixture into the oil. Do not overcrowd with too much at once in the oil as this will reduce the temperature of the oil. Fry until golden brown and crispy. Drain on kitchen paper and serve immediately with my avocado raita.

# GARLIC AND CHILLI CASSAVA ROASTIES

If you want a different starch to replace potatoes, you should consider roasting cassava. It's a root vegetable also known as yucca or mogo. These roasties are crunchy and melt in the mouth and will jazz up any roast dinner!

**SERVES 4**

## INGREDIENTS

- *500g frozen cassava (mogo)*
- *3 tbsp chilli garlic oil*
- *2 tbsp red chilli powder*
- *1 bulb of garlic (roughly 10-12 garlic pieces), blended to a paste*
- *1 tbsp onion powder*
- *1 tbsp paprika*
- *2 tsp salt*
- *Juice of ½ lemon*
- *Water for boiling*

## METHOD

Boil the cassava in a large pan of boiling water for approx. 20 minutes. Poke with a knife to check they are cooked through.

In a bowl mix together the chilli powder, onion powder, paprika, and salt. Now add the blended garlic and chilli garlic oil and lemon juice. Drain the cassava and pour the spice mix over the cassava. Save 1 tsp of the spice mix for later. Toss both parts together gently ensuring not to break any of the cassava.

Cook in a preheated oven of 220 degrees for 35-40 minutes until they are crispy and golden on the outside, soft and fluffy on the inside. Transfer to a large bowl and toss through that 1 tsp of spice mix you saved earlier. Delicious on their own or as an accompaniment to your favourite Sunday roast!

# CORN ON THE COB WITH CHILLI & LIME

This is undoubtedly the most delicious way to cook corn on the cob. The simple flavours bring this easy recipe to life! This appetiser reminds me of my school holidays to India. There would be a Lari (food cart) on every corner selling these juicy, fresh, steaming hot, charred on barbeque giant corn on the cobs. Smothered in butter, chilli, salt and lime. Alternatively, you can just as easily grill the cobs if barbequing is not an option.

**SERVES 2-4**

## INGREDIENTS

- *4 corn cobs*
- *2 limes cut into halves*
- *½ tsp salt*
- *½ tsp red chilli powder*
- *4 knobs of butter*

## METHOD

Firstly, wash and clean the corn cobs peeling away any silks. Wipe clean. Place under a hot grill/on a bbq, turning occasionally. Cook so they are golden and charred evenly on all sides.

Now in a bowl make the spice rub by mixing together the salt and red chilli powder.

Generously butter the golden grilled corn. Dip one half of the lime wedges into the chilli salt rub. Rub the coated lime over the buttery cob, squeezing the lime at the same time. Dip the lime into the rub again if required. All that's left to do is to take a great big bite into the buttery, salty, spicy and zesty corn.

TINDORA BATETA

# TINDORA BATETA

Tindora translated is Ivy Gourd, also known as baby watermelon. A lightly spiced vegetable dish coupled with bateta (potatoes), it's an extremely easy dish to whip up with basic spices. This is my most favourite Indian vegetable of all time. A minimal effort recipe to add to your weeknight meals.

**SERVES 4**

## INGREDIENTS

- *450g tindora (ivy gourd)*
- *1 medium potato*
- *4 tbsp sunflower oil + 1 tbsp for the potatoes*
- *1 ½ tsp black mustard seeds*
- *1/8 tsp asafoetida*
- *¼ tsp turmeric + ¼ tsp for the potatoes*
- *¾ tsp salt, or to taste + ¼ tsp for the potatoes*
- *1 tsp garlic paste*
- *1 tsp green chilli paste*
- *½ tsp dry coriander powder*
- *Chopped fresh coriander for garnish*

## METHOD

Wash the tindora well in salty water and dry them with a dish cloth. Top and tail each tindora, being careful not to take too much off each end. Slice each one in half lengthways and then each half into quarters in the same lengthways direction. So, you should get approx. 8 slices from each tindora. Set to one side.

Wash and peel the potato and cut the potato into similar long rectangle shapes to the tindora pieces, but twice the thickness.

Now the prep is done let's start with cooking the tindora first. In a large non-stick frying pan/wok add 4 tbsp sunflower oil and place on a medium heat. Add the mustard seeds, and as they start to pop add the asafoetida and turn the heat right down to low. Now add the chopped tindora and mix well with the tempered mustard seeds. Add the salt and stir fry on a medium heat for 5 minutes. Now cover for 15 minutes with a lid to steam cook the tindora, stirring occasionally.

In the meantime, you can cook the potatoes. In a small frying pan heat 1 tbsp sunflower oil on medium heat and add the chopped potatoes. Stir well so the potatoes are coated in the oil. Add the ¼ tsp turmeric and mix well so the potatoes turn a beautiful shade of amber. Now add the dry coriander powder and ¼ tsp salt and cook the potatoes until they are ¾ of the way cooked through.

Check on the tindora, they should be cooking away nicely. Now add the potatoes to the tindora and gently stir both veggies together. Stir in the garlic and green chilli pastes, along with the turmeric. Cook for a further 10 minutes until the potatoes are cooked through. The tindora should also be cooked by this stage. They will still have a slight crunch to them which is perfect. Just how they should be. Finish by garnishing with fresh coriander and serve with fresh warm chapati. I like to make a wrap: fill a chapati with the tindora and bateta nu shaak. Yum!

# BHINDA NI KHADI (OKRA IN A SPICY YOGURT SOUP)

This is an Indian yogurt soup cooked with chickpea flour and okra. Another great winter warmer. This is a comforting and satisfying soup that really hits the spot. It's seasoned with lots of other ingredients to make it warming and delicious.

This dish is a 2 step process. You first need to sauté the okra in a pan until it's slightly crisp then add it to the khadi.

**SERVES 4**

## INGREDIENTS

### Ingredients for the Bhinda

- *450g of Bhindi/Okra, or you can use frozen but you need thaw them and pat them dry of any water*
- *2 tbsp sunflower oil*
- *6-7 fenugreek seeds*
- *½ tsp black mustard seeds*
- *1/8 tsp asafoetida*
- *½ tsp ghee*
- *¾ tsp salt, or to taste*
- *1 tsp garlic paste*
- *½ tsp green chilli paste*
- *1 tsp dry coriander powder*
- *¼ tsp turmeric*

### Ingredients for the Khadi *(page 26)*

## METHOD

Wash the okra in salt water and pat dry with a tea towel. Top and tail each okra then slice into rings. Each ring should be less than 1cm in thickness. You don't want them too thin or too thick.

Heat the sunflower oil on medium heat in a large frying pan, Now add the mustard seeds and fenugreek seeds. Put a lid on the pan and when you hear the mustard seeds start to pop turn the heat right down and add the asafoetida. Sauté for a few seconds then add the okra and mix with the tempered spices. Add the ghee. This helps to take away the stickiness of the okra. Cook on a medium heat for 15 minutes before adding the turmeric, salt, garlic and green chilli pastes. Mix and combine well with the okra. Stir fry over a medium-high heat for 10 minutes, stirring often to prevent the okras from burning and sticking to the pan. You will see the okra pieces start to shrink in size slightly and become a much deeper and darker green colour. I like mine with a crispy bite. Now add the dry coriander and cook for a couple more minutes. Take off the heat and place to one side for later. You can eat this okra as it is. We call this bhinda nu shaak and it goes perfectly with fresh warm chapatis. However, this recipe calls for a yogurt based soup called khadi that is a match made in heaven with my bhinda nu shaak.

Prepare the Khadi as my recipe suggests on *page 26*

Add the cooked okra to your khadi and simmer gently over a low heat for 10 minutes to allow all the spices from both dishes to infuse together. Serve while it's warm and soak up all that warm soupy goodness with chapatis.

# CORN ON THE COB CURRY

This corn on the cob curry is unique and so easy to make. Fresh sweetcorn is steamed then simmered in a delicious onion, garlic and tomato gravy. This gravy poured over plain white rice is divine. It's finger licking and delicious.

**SERVES 2**

## INGREDIENTS

- *2 large corn on cobs, slice each cob one into 4-5 equal slices*
- *1 medium potato, cut into 6 equally sized chunks*
- *2 tbsp sunflower oil*
- *2 cinnamon sticks*
- *3-4 cloves*
- *Pinch of asafoetida*
- *1 onion, finely chopped*
- *1 tomato, finely chopped*
- *½ tsp garlic paste*
- *½ tsp red chilli powder*
- *¼ tsp green chilli paste*
- *1 tsp coriander powder*
- *¼ tsp garam masala*
- *½ tsp salt, or to taste*
- *Chopped fresh coriander for garnish*

## METHOD

In a medium sized pressure cooker add the sliced corn cobs, fill ¾ of the cooker with water. Place the chopped potato on top of the corn and pressure cook for 6 whistles.

In a separate saucepan on medium heat, add the oil, asafoetida, cinnamon sticks and cloves. Let them sizzle and then add the chopped onions. Sauté until they become soft and translucent. Then add the finely chopped tomato and cook until the tomatoes soften, and the oil starts to separate at the edges of the mix. Add the garlic paste, red chilli powder, green chilli paste, coriander powder and garam masala. Stir all the spices together with the onion and tomato mixture. Now add the pressure-cooked corn cobs into the saucepan and mix all together well. Add the cooked potatoes to the saucepan along with 400ml of the starchy water from the pressure cooker. Stir everything gently so the potatoes don't break. Simmer on a low heat for 10 minutes and garnish with coriander. Serve with bhatura, naan or parathas and matar pilau rice. All that delicious sauce and the juices from the corn taste incredible poured over matar pilau rice.

# BATETA POHA

A perfect breakfast/brunch dish made from poha (rice) and bateta (potatoes). In India this is a popular breakfast dish and growing up we would make this for lunch too! Poha is made by flattening rice. The Poha benefits from being lactose and fat free so makes a healthy dish. This dish brings delicious tastes and textures of spiciness from the chillies, sweetness from the raisins and crunchiness from the peanuts and cashews. There is also a tanginess from the lemon and then the potatoes further enhance the textures. It will be like a celebration of all different kinds of flavours in your mouth!

**SERVES 4**

## INGREDIENTS

- *2 medium potatoes, peeled and diced into cm cubes*
- *150g of Poha (flat rice)*
- *1 tsp ginger paste*
- *1 tsp garlic paste*
- *¾ tsp green chilli paste*
- *½ tsp granulated sugar*
- *¼ lemon juice*
- *4 tbsp sunflower oil*
- *¾ tsp salt, or to taste*
- *½ tsp turmeric*
- *½ tsp whole cumin seeds*
- *1 tsp sesame seeds*
- *2 tbsp of chopped unsalted peanuts*
- *2-3 tbsp toasted cashews for garnish*
- *2-3 tbsp green raisins for garnish*
- *1-2 tbsp fresh pomegranate for garnish*

## METHOD

First of all, gently wash the poha in a colander. Be careful not to break up the poha flakes. They will soften with the water. Leave in the colander for all the water to drain out whilst you start to cook the rest of the ingredients.

In a large wok heat the oil on a medium-low heat and add the cumin. Wait for them to sizzle and release a wonderful aroma before adding the diced potatoes. Stir and add the chopped peanuts. Once the potatoes look/feel like they are ¾ of the way cooked through add the garlic, ginger and green chilli pastes, turmeric, salt and sesame seeds. Mix gently so you don't break up the potatoes. Now add the washed and drained poha and mix, fully combining the poha with the potatoes. Now add the sugar and the juice of ¼ lemon and stir through gently. Cook for around 5-10 mins until the potatoes are fully cooked but not mushy. Serve with a garnish of the raisins and toasted cashews, and a sprinkling of pomegranate. Prepare for an explosion or flavours and textures in your mouth!

BHARELI BI[illegible]AIYA (STUFFED OKRA'S)

# BHARELI BINDA RAVAIYA (STUFFED OKRAS)

The okras are stuffed with an exciting sesame, peanut and coriander mixture. Cooked until the stuffing is crispy and golden. An irresistible dish of fresh okras that will enlighten your tastebuds with every bite. It's outright delicious

I loved eating this dish growing up and I remember whilst my mum was cooking them I'd sneakily pick some out of the pan to eat. This is not something I can personally eat as a main meal. It's more of a side dish, or in my case more of an excuse to go into the kitchen and snack on them throughout the day.

**SERVES 2**

## INGREDIENTS

- *200g whole okra (approx. 20 pieces)*
- *1 tbsp sunflower oil*

### Ingredients for the stuffing

- *4 ½ tbsp gram flour*
- *1 ½ tbsp coriander powder*
- *1 tbsp sesame seeds*
- *2 tsp ground peanuts*
- *¼ tsp turmeric*
- *½ tsp salt, or to taste*
- *½ tsp garlic paste*
- *1 tsp green chilli paste*
- *½ tsp granulated sugar*
- *¼ tsp bicarbonate soda*
- *Pinch of asafoetida*
- *5 tbsp sunflower oil*

## METHOD

In a mixing bowl add all the ingredients (leaving out the oil) for the ravaiya stuffing. Use your fingertips to combine all the ingredients together well (wear disposable gloves if you prefer). Now add the sunflower oil and mix together well with the spices.

Now wash your okras in warm salty water and use a damp towel to wipe them clean. Top and tail both ends of the okras. Make a slit lengthways down the middle of the okras, careful not to cut right through. Just enough so you can still stuff them.

Now carefully stuff each okra with the ravaiya stuffing mix you made and put them to one side in a plate.

Put 1 tbsp of cooking oil in a frying pan and heat on a medium-low heat. Now carefully place each okra one by one in the frying pan. Crumble over in the pan any leftover ravaiya stuffing mix. This will turn crispy and nutty during cooking. Cover the pan and continue to cook on a low heat, delicately turning the okras occasionally so they don't burn but do cook equally on all sides. Cook until the okras turn a dark green colour and the stuffing has turned crispy.

Can be eaten with any Indian bread, or served as a side to any main meal.

# RINGAN & BETETA RAVAIYA (STUFFED AUBERGINE AND POTATO)

The ultimate vegan comfort dish made by stuffing aubergines with a taste tantalising peanut based masala. Ravaiya means stuffed. Any stuffed vegetable is called a ravaiya. The masala stuffing is made with gram flour, crushed peanuts, Indian spices, ginger, garlic and fresh coriander. As a child I used to hate aubergines because of their slimy texture. As I've grown older I've learned to appreciate the humble aubergine and this has to be one of my most satisfying vegetarian dishes. This is my mum's recipe which I will cherish forever. If I were to ask my dad what he'd like to eat this dish would be at the top of his list with fresh warm chapatis.

**SERVES 2**

## INGREDIENTS

- *4 baby Aubergines (make sure they are light in weight as this means they contain less pips inside)*
- *2 small potatoes, cut into equal quarters*

### Ingredients for the stuffing

- *1 tsp gram flour*
- *2 ½ tsp ground coriander*
- *1 tsp coarsely chopped peanuts*
- *3 tsp ground peanuts*
- *1 ½ tsp red chilli powder*
- *1 tsp salt, or to taste*
- *1 tsp garlic paste*
- *1 tsp ginger paste*
- *1 heaped tbsp jaggery*
- *¼ tsp bicarbonate soda*
- *½ tsp turmeric*
- *1 tsp granulated sugar*
- *4 tbsp sunflower oil*
- *2 tbsp freshly chopped coriander + extra for garnishing at the end.*

## METHOD

First let's make the ravaiya stuffing. In a bowl combine all the ingredients listed for the stuffing. Using your fingertips (wear disposable gloves if you've just had your nails done), combine all the ingredients together by rubbing between your fingers and breaking down the jaggery so all the spices can infuse together.

In a separate last mixing bowl, wash your aubergines well in warm salty water. Trim the tops of the aubergines but leave a little bit of the stalk as it helps to hold the shape of the aubergine during cooking. Make 2 slits in each of the aubergines, creating a crosscut. Make the slits as deep as ¾ of the way down the aubergine leaving the stalk uncut.

Now carefully stuff your prepped baby aubergines with the ravaiya stuffing. Stuff as much as you can in without breaking/splitting the aubergine in half. Place each stuffed baby aubergine in a large saucepan. If you have stuffing left in your bowl, just add it to the saucepan. Now fill 1/3 of the saucepan with warm water. Now place the pan on medium to high heat and bring to the boil. Once it starts bubbling away, reduce the heat to low and simmer for 20 minutes with the lid on. Now add the quartered potatoes to the saucepan and continue to simmer without the lid. Cook for a further 20-25 minutes until the water has reduced to a beautiful rusty coloured thick sauce. At this point the aubergines and potatoes will be perfectly cooked. Turn off the heat and garnish with coriander.

Serve with chapati and a simple kachumber salad. If you really want to make a feast out it, I highly recommend you have this dish with my yellow toor dal khichdi *(page 171)* and khadi *(page 26)*.

POTATO BHAJIA

# POTATO BHAJIA

Bhajia are also known as fritters and there must be hundreds of different varieties which you can make out of anything! It's an addictive obsession. You can use this same recipe to fry all different veggies such as onion rings, sweet potato, yam, baby corn, cauliflower and even chillies! Dipped in tomato ketchup is as simple as it gets or go crazy and have it in a sandwich. It's an ideal evening snack or with a cup of chai. There is something about whipping up some quick bhajia's like these when it's raining outside. I think it's an Indian thing, eating them during a storm – it just makes the whole experience more enjoyable and satisfying. Nothing can beat a hot and crispy bhajia.

**SERVES 4**

## INGREDIENTS

- *2 medium sized king Edward potatoes*
- *200g chickpea flour*
- *1 tbsp rice flour (makes the bhajia crispy)*
- *1 tbsp sunflower*
- *½ tsp sea salt*
- *½ tsp red chilli powder*
- *½ tsp green chilli paste*
- *½ tsp crushed black peppercorns*
- *½ tsp course crushed coriander seeds*
- *130ml warm water*
- *Oil for deep frying*

## METHOD

Peel the skin off the potatoes. Using a mandolin slicer, slice the potatoes with 1/2cm depth, rinse with cold water (to remove excess starch), and spread out on some tissue paper to soak up any excess moisture.

To prepare the batter, in a mixing bowl, add the chickpea flour, rice flour oil, sea salt, red chilli powder and green chilli paste. Combine all the spices well with the flour. Now add the water and whisk all the ingredients together in a clockwise direction to form a smooth batter with no lumps. Rest the batter for 30 minutes.

Heat oil in a wok for deep frying. Check the oil is hot enough by dropping a little portion of the batter into the oil. The batter must rise steadily to the top without browning too quickly. This is the correct temperature (approx. 180 degrees). If it comes up too quick,ly then your oil is too hot. If the batter settles down at the bottom of the pan, then it's not hot enough.

Add a tablespoon of this hot oil to the batter mixture – this adds a nice gloss to the bhajias.

Now dip the potato slices in the batter one by one fully coating each slice. Sprinkle with crushed black peppercorns and crushed coriander seeds. Deep fry in the hot oil until they puff up and turn beautifully golden yellow in colour. Flip and fry the bhajia on both sides. Remember to keep the flame on medium heat to give the potato a chance to fully cook.

Once cooked, remove and transfer the fried bhajias to tissue paper to absorb any excess oil. Serve with my coriander and garlic raita.

GREEN MUNG DAL

# GREEN MUNG DAL

We call this Monday Mung Day in our house – not only is it a tradition passed on from generations but, it also kicks off the week to a healthy start, boosting those iron levels to get us through the week! Create this sensational dish in less than half an hour with minimum ingredients but maximum flavour. I can never get enough of green mung dal because it's light but hearty and the kids love a bowl of hot mung dal on a cold winter night!

**SERVES 4**

## INGREDIENTS

- *350g green mung dal*
- *1 tbsp toor dal*
- *2 tbsp sunflower oil*
- *2 tsp black mustard seeds*
- *¼ tsp asafoetida*
- *½ tsp turmeric*
- *3-4 curry leaves*
- *2 dry Kashmiri red chillies*
- *3 tomatoes, finely chopped*
- *2 tsp dry coriander*
- *1 ½ tsp salt, or to taste*
- *1 ½ tsp garlic paste*
- *1 tsp ginger paste*
- *1 ½ tsp red chilli powder*
- *1 tsp garam masala*
- *Juice of ¼ lemon*
- *100ml water*
- *Chopped fresh coriander for garnish*

## METHOD

In a pressure cooker add the green mung dal and the toor dal. Fill your cooker with water at least 2 inches above the level of the dals. Cook for 15 minutes, or 3 whistles worth. If you don't have a pressure cooker, don't worry, you can simply boil the dals in a large saucepan with water until they are cooked. Allow an additional 50-60 minutes of cooking time for this.

You don't want a mushy mung dal. It should still hold its shape and be slightly al dente. Adjust cooking times according to your pressure cooker.

Once your dal is cooked, set to one side. In a large saucepan, heat the oil, the mustard seeds and dry red chillies on a high heat with the lid on. Once you hear the seeds start to pop turn the heat right down and add the asafoetida and curry leaves. Keeping the lid on, give the spices in the pan a swirl around the pan. Once the popping slows down remove the lid and add the turmeric and swirl through the oil. Add the chopped tomatoes and cook them down for 10 minutes. Now add the dry coriander, salt, garlic and ginger pastes, red chilli powder and garam masala. Mix everything together well. Allow all the spices to infuse together well for a minute or so. Now add the cooked mung dal to the saucepan and combine all the spices well with the dal. Add 100ml of water, stir and simmer on a low heat for 10 minutes. Squeeze over the juice of ¼ lemon and garnish with coriander. Serve with chapati or pilau rice.

# CHANA CHOLE (CHICKPEA CURRY)

I married a man who loves meat curries, chicken curry, lamb curry, fish curry, anything non veg! He would eat chicken curry for breakfast, lunch and dinner if he could. Nevertheless, he loves all the food I cook, especially this chana chole, which is his favourite vegetarian curry. (It must be because it smells like chicken curry). To be honest, my children love this meal too, minus the chilli. A super flexible and adaptable nutritious dish for the whole family.

**SERVES 2**

## INGREDIENTS

- *1 onion blended to a mush*
- *350g passata*
- *1 tin white chickpeas (400g)*
- *1/8 tsp of asafoetida*
- *1 cinnamon stick*
- *10 cashew nuts – grounded with pestle and mortar*
- *1 ½ tsp garlic paste*
- *1 tsp ginger paste*
- *1 tsp salt, or to taste*
- *2 tsp tomato puree*
- *3 tbsp sunflower oil*
- *½ tsp turmeric*
- *1 ½ tsp red chilli powder*
- *½ tsp garam masala*
- *1 tsp granulated sugar*
- *50ml water*
- *Chopped fresh coriander for garnish*

## METHOD

In a large saucepan heat the oil, add the cinnamon stick and the asafoetida. Let the cinnamon sizzle and release that beautiful aroma before adding the blended onions. Cook the onions on a low heat until browned. Stir regularly otherwise the onions will stick and burn. Once the onions have browned add tomato puree, stir and cook for a couple of minutes before adding the garlic, ginger, turmeric, red chilli powder, sugar, garam masala and salt. Mix all the ingredients together well with the onions and tomato puree. Sauté for a few minutes and add the passata and water. Stir and add the grounded cashews. Cook and stir occasionally until you see the oil rise to the surface of the tomato sauce. Drain the tin of chickpeas. Take a small handful (approx. 10 chickpeas) and mush them with your hands and add to the sauce in the pan. This will help to thicken the sauce slightly. Add the rest of the chickpeas and cook on a low heat for around 15 minutes. Garnish with fresh coriander. Serve with Jeera Rice and Bhatura Puris.

RINGAN, BATETA AND TUVAR NU SHA

# RINGAN, BATETA AND TUVAR NU SHAAK (AUBERGINE, POTATO AND PIGEON PEA CURRY)

Ever wondered how you can incorporate aubergine into your diet? This transports the flavour of a bland veg into something sensational, believe me! It's a very flavoursome mix which has lots of textures and is a true reflection on the Gujarati cuisine. It was that special it was served at my wedding.

**SERVES 4**

## INGREDIENTS

- *4 baby aubergines or 1 large aubergine*
- *2 medium sized potatoes*
- *1 finely chopped tomato*
- *Handful of pigeon peas. You can also use regular garden peas*
- *3 tbsp sunflower oil*
- *1 tsp whole cumin*
- *1/8 tsp asafoetida*
- *½ tsp turmeric*
- *1 tsp ginger paste*
- *½ tsp garlic paste*
- *½ tsp green chilli paste*
- *¼ tsp red chilli powder*
- *1 ½ tsp coriander powder*
- *½ inch sized piece of jaggery or 1 tsp brown sugar*
- *1 tsp salt, or to taste*
- *50ml water*
- *Chopped fresh coriander for garnish*

## METHOD

Cut the aubergine and potatoes into inch sized chunks and put to one side. Heat the oil in a saucepan on a medium heat and add the cumin seeds. Stir for a few seconds until they are sizzling, and the aroma is released. Now add the asafoetida, turmeric and the chopped aubergine and potatoes. Add the pigeon peas and the chopped tomatoes, turn the heat down and stir. Now you can add the remaining ingredients apart from the water and fresh coriander. Mix all the ingredients together well. Let all the spices infuse into the veggies for a few minutes before adding the water. Put the lid on the pan and simmer on a low heat, stirring occasionally. Once the aubergine has softened and potatoes are cooked, garnish with coriander and serve.

# PAV BHAJI

This dish definitely serves up your 5 a day. It is one of the most popular street food dishes which can literally be found on all restaurant menus across India because it guarantees satisfaction! A colourful smash of vegetables sautéed to bring out the most delicious taste and aroma with a handful of spices. The sprinkle of onions, coriander and lemon gives that final zing which leaves you wanting more! Here's a little secret it tastes even better the next day as a spread on a slice of bread! Perfect for a lunch treat!

**SERVES 4**

## INGREDIENTS

- *2 finely diced onions*
- *5 blended tomatoes*
- *3 medium potatoes boiled with skin on to retain the moisture. Peel the skin off once boiled.*
- *¼ cauliflower boiled/steamed*
- *2 handfuls of garden peas boiled/steamed*
- *100ml of sunflower oil*
- *½ tsp asafoetida*
- *1 tbsp tomato puree*
- *Garlic paste*
- *Red chilli powder*
- *Garam masala*
- *Turmeric*
- *1 tsp Sugar*
- *Salt, or to taste*
- *¼ freshly squeezed lemon juice*
- *Chopped fresh coriander for garnish*
- *4 fresh soft bread rolls*

## METHOD

In large karahi or wok heat the oil on a medium to high heat and add the asafoetida, reduce the heat to a medium-low flame and add the onions. Cook until light brown in colour. Add the blended tomatoes and tomato puree. Mix and cook until the oil separates from the mixtures. This initial process of the method will take a good 20-30 minutes. Mix in the garlic, red chilli powder, garam masala, turmeric, salt and lemon juice. Cook for a further 5 minutes on low heat. Stirring occasionally, whilst this is cooking, with your hands mush the cauliflower and the peas in a bowl. Now would be a good time to take out a couple of tablespoons of this mixture to use later when toasting the bread rolls. Add the mushed cauliflower and peas and stir well. Mush the potatoes by hand and add to the pan. Mix everything well together. Now with a masher, mash all the ingredients in the pan whilst cooking. You still want to keep some consistency and bite to the bhaji so don't mush to puree. Cook for a further 10-15 minutes to enable all the ingredients to infuse together, stirring regularly. Garnish with coriander to finish the bhaji off. Now for the pav/bread rolls. Heat a frying pan/griddle pan. Whilst the pan is heating up, slice the rolls in half and spread with salted butter. Toast both sides of rolls in the heated pan on a medium heat. Once they start to brown and crisp up, spread on a very thin layer of the bhaji mixture you put to one side earlier. Cook the rolls in the pan for a further minute or so on low heat.

The Pav Bhaji is now ready. When serving, garnish with a sprinkling of diced red onion, thinly sliced green chillies, and fresh coriander. Serve the bhaji hot with the freshly toasted pav (bread rolls).

ALOO MATAR

# ALOO MATAR (TOMATO, PEAS AND POTATO CURRY)

This is a meal I remember very well growing up. When I'd get home from school I'd always go in the kitchen and lift the lids of all the pans to check what my mum had cooked for dinner. If I saw it was aloo matar, I'd get excited and go get washed and changed as quickly as possible. I absolutely loved this meal growing up. The sweetness of the tomatoes in this dish really balances out the spices. One of my all-time favourites. I guarantee you will fall in love with this simple delightful meal. Best served with plain basmati rice or chapatis to soak up all that delicious, spicy, saucy goodness.

**SERVES 4**

## INGREDIENTS

- *6 ripe tomatoes*
- *2 medium potatoes*
- *80g garden peas (fresh or frozen)*
- *4 tbsp sunflower oil*
- *1 tsp mustard seeds*
- *½ tsp turmeric*
- *½ tsp coriander powder*
- *1 tsp red chilli powder*
- *2 tsp granulated sugar*
- *1 tsp garlic paste*
- *½ tsp ginger paste*
- *½ tsp salt, or to taste*
- *Chopped fresh coriander for garnish*

## METHOD

This is very much a one pot meal. I like to chop and prepare all the ingredients in one big bowl ready to add to the sizzling pan.

In a large bowl, chop the potatoes and tomatoes into small 1cm chunks. Add to the bowl peas, ginger paste, garlic paste, sugar, red chilli powder, coriander powder, turmeric and salt.

In a large saucepan, heat the oil on a high heat and add the mustard seeds, put the lid on. Once you start to hear the mustard seeds popping turn the heat right down. As the popping starts to slow down you can add the bowl of ingredient you prepared above. Give it a good mix ensuring all spices are mixed well with the vegetables. You don't need to add any water as the tomatoes will release their own juices. Let it cook on a medium to low heat with the lid on, stirring occasionally. Cook until the potatoes are cooked through but keeping their shape. Garnish with coriander.

ALOO METHI

# ALOO METHI

Methi has a strong definition but swirled together with potatoes and ginger brings a completely new sensation to the pallet. The bitterness of the methi is taken back with seasoning from a handful of spices.

**SERVES 2**

## INGREDIENTS

- *4 medium sized skin on boiled potatoes – I like to use king Edward potatoes. Any potatoes with red eyes will work.*
- *150g freshly chopped fenugreek leaves (methi)*
- *2 tbsp mustard oil*
- *½ tsp turmeric*
- *¼ tsp asafoetida*
- *1 tsp ginger paste*
- *1 ½ tsp garlic*
- *½ tsp green chilli paste*
- *1 tsp dry coriander*
- *½ tsp whole cumin seeds*
- *½ tsp salt or to taste*
- *¼ tsp dry mango powder, or squeeze of lemon*

## METHOD

Peel the skin off the potatoes and dice into 1 inch chunks. Set aside.

Heat the mustard oil until it's really hot on a high flame. Lower the flame, add the cumin seeds and let them sizzle for half a minute or so. Add the asafoetida. Now add the garlic and ginger pastes, and sauté for a few seconds ensuring not to burn it. Now add the chopped potatoes and dry coriander. Stir until combined. Add the green chilli paste and stir well.

Fry the potatoes for 5-6 minutes on a medium flame until they turn slightly golden.

Now add the chopped fenugreek (methi) leaves and stir. Add in the turmeric and salt.

Stir on a low heat until the leaves have wilted. Add dry mango powder and stir. This will add a slight tartness to the dish. If you can't get any mango powder, use a squeeze of lemon instead.

Serve Aloo Methi with chapati.

If you like the taste of methi leaves, for a stronger flavour add more to my recipe to suit your taste buds.

ALOO GOBI WITH PEAS

# ALOO GOBI WITH PEAS

Cauliflower lovers will be in their element with this dish which also satisfies carb cravings. Potatoes, cauliflower and peas folded in cumin, chilli and garlic. A flash of flavours with a subtle sweetness from the petis pois.

**SERVES 4**

## INGREDIENTS

- *Medium sized cauliflower*
- *2 medium sized king Edward potatoes*
- *150g shelled garden peas*
- *2 tbsp oil*
- *1 tsp mustard seeds*
- *1 tsp whole cumin*
- *½ tsp turmeric*
- *¾ tsp garlic, minced*
- *1 tsp green chillies, minced (adjust the heat according to personal preference)*
- *1 tsp salt, or to taste*
- *Chopped fresh coriander for garnish*

## METHOD

Cut the cauliflower and potatoes roughly into 1cm chunks. You can cut them bigger than this, however you will need to adjust cooking times as bigger chunks will take longer to cook.

Heat the oil in a non-stick frying pan on a high heat. Add the mustard seeds and cumin seeds. As you start to hear the mustard seeds popping, turn the heat right down. Once the popping slows down add the potatoes and cook on a medium-low heat for 5 mins. Now add the cauliflower and the turmeric. Mix the potatoes and cauliflower thoroughly. Add half of the salt now as it helps speed up the cooking of the cauliflower. Put the lid back on the pan, stirring often. Poke the potatoes with a spoon. If they look and feel like they are nearly cooked, add the petit pois, minced green chilli and garlic and, the rest of the salt. Give it a good mix to evenly coat the potatoes, cauliflower and peas in the garlic and chilli paste. Further cook with the lid off until the potatoes are cooked through. You don't want a mushy potato. The cauliflower should be cooked but still have a slight crunch. Garnish with coriander and serve with chapatis. Also, goes well with Dal Bhat *(page 48)* and cucumber raita *(page 190)*

Tastes great with a salad the next day for lunch! Or in a toastie!

CUMIN POTATO SHAAK

# CUMIN POTATO SHAAK

This is the real Bombay potato! A simple blend of spices tossed between chopped potatoes. A delicious alternative to a midweek treat which satisfies those carb cravings.

**SERVES 4**

## INGREDIENTS

- *5 medium sized king Edward potatoes*
- *2 tbsp sunflower oil*
- *2 tsp mustard seeds*
- *1 tsp whole cumin seeds*
- *1 tsp turmeric*
- *2 tsp dry coriander*
- *½ tsp salt*
- *1 tsp red chilli powder*

## METHOD

Cut the potatoes into little square bite sized pieces.

In a non stick frying pan heat the oil for a couple of minutes on a low heat. Add the mustard and cumin seeds and, turn the gas up to a high flame. Once the popping of the seeds slows down, turn the heat right down otherwise you'll burn rather than temper the seeds. Next add the turmeric, put the lid back on and swirl around. Lift the lid slightly and add a handful of the potatoes, then close the lid to avoid back splash of the oil. After a few seconds lift the lid completely and add the rest of the potatoes and give a good stir ensuring all that vibrant turmeric coloured oil fully coats the potatoes. A lot of Indian cooks add the turmeric after adding all other ingredients, but I don't think it covers the food as evenly as it does adding it to the oil like in this recipe. Now add the dry coriander and mix well. Cook on medium-low heat, stirring often to ensure the potatoes don't burn. After about 20-25 minutes the potatoes should start to soften and break if you cut with the end of a spoon. You don't want them mushy! When you get to this point add the salt and red chilli powder. Toss the potatoes around the pan well so the salt and chilli powder are evenly distributed. Cover with the lid for a few minutes on a low flame. Garnish with coriander and you're ready to serve. Perfect with bakri.

Leftovers are the best the day after. Put the potato shaak in a slice of buttered bread with ketchup. The perfect Indian chip butty.

# MASALA BEANS

This a perfect meat free dish, which is at the top of my list when it comes to a quick and tasty meal. One the whole family can enjoy together. When the spices infuse with the baked beans you will not believe the taste you have just created. We don't eat baked beans any other way in our house.

**SERVES 2**

## INGREDIENTS

- *415g tinned baked beans*
- *Half of a white onion*
- *1 tsp sunflower oil*
- *1 tsp mustard seeds*
- *½ tsp turmeric*
- *½ tsp ground coriander*
- *½ tsp garam masala*
- *¼ tsp salt*
- *½ tsp garlic paste*
- *½ tsp green chilli paste*
- *Chopped fresh coriander for garnish*

## METHOD

Cook on a medium-high heat, add oil in a saucepan. Add the mustard seeds and cover the lid. Keep on a medium-high heat. Once you hear the mustard seeds start to pop turn the heat right down. It's like waiting for popcorn to slow down popping in the microwave. Once you hear the mustard seeds popping has slowed down, it's time to add the baked beans. Add a large spoonful of beans in to start and put the lid back on the pan, otherwise the mustard seeds have a tendency to splat back at you. You can now safely lift the lid and add the rest of the tin of beans. Keep it on a low heat while you add the other ingredients. Add the turmeric, salt, dry coriander and stir. Now add the minced garlic and green chilli paste. Give it a good mix. Keep the gas on low stirring occasionally. After about 10 minutes the beans should be bubbling nicely. Make sure they don't stick to the pan. To finish, add the garam masala, chopped coriander and stir. Serve with fresh warm chapatis. Such a quick and easy weeknight recipe. Simple yet so yummy! Also, delicious poured over a jacket potato with grated mature cheddar for lunch!

One with onion and one without onion for the fussy people in my family...and it's not the children...it's the hubby!

# CHICKEN

# CHICKEN MASALA

This is a classic chicken curry in all its unpretentious glory. I feel like you can eat delicious food from all around the world, but you still need a lip smacking chicken curry to feel like you've really eaten! As well as being a flavour packed curry, it is a winner with the whole family. My kids love it too. I like to cook this on a low heat for a couple of hours so I tend to make this on the weekend. It also freezes well if you want to batch cook.

**SERVES 4**

## INGREDIENTS

- *500g boneless skinless chicken thigh, cut into bitesize chunks*
- *500g on the bone skinless chicken thigh, cut into bitesize chunks*
- *6 tbsp sunflower oil*
- *2 inch cinnamon stick*
- *5-6 cloves*
- *4 cardamon pods*
- *3 white onions, finely chopped*
- *400g passata*
- *100ml water*
- *2 ½ tsp garlic paste*
- *2 ½ tsp ginger paste*
- *1 ½ tsp turmeric*
- *2 ½ tsp dry coriander*
- *2 ½ tsp dry cumin*
- *1 tbsp Kashmiri chilli powder*
- *1 ½ tsp red chilli powder*
- *1 tsp garam masala + ½ tsp to add at the end of cooking*
- *1 ½ tsp salt*
- *½ tsp lemon juice*
- *Freshly chopped coriander for garnish*

## METHOD

In a deep, large pan heat sunflower oil on a medium heat. Add cinnamon stick, cloves and cardamon pods. Let them sizzle before adding the finely chopped onions. You want to caramelise the onions until they are brown in colour. Turn the heat down to low and add the passata. Stir well with the onions. Add water and continue to cook on a low heat stirring occasionally. Once you see the oil start to separate from the onion/tomato mix you can add the spices. Add garlic and ginger pastes, turmeric, dry coriander and cumin, Kashmiri chilli powder, red chilli powder, 1 tsp of the garam masala, salt and lemon juice. Mix everything together well incorporating all the spices into the tomato base. Allow this to cook for a few minutes before adding the chicken. Ensure all the chicken is coated well with the curry base. Now put the lid on the pan and continue to cook on a very low heat for approx. 2 hours or, until the chicken is cooked, juicy, tender and falling off the bone. Add a final seasoning of garam masala, ½ tsp, and a garnish of coriander.

You can also add potatoes to this curry. If so, add peeled baby potatoes around two thirds of the way into cooking the chicken.

Enjoy this delicious warming chicken curry with naan or chapatis and rice. You'll definitely go back for seconds.

# 10 MINUTE CHICKEN CURRY

This is a fast pace chicken curry without compromising on taste. I use chicken breast in the recipe as it is quicker than thigh. This dish originated from my husband's essential non veg curry fix, as it's quick and easy to whip up.

**SERVES 2**

## INGREDIENTS

- *300g chicken breast, chopped into bitesize pieces*
- *130g of tinned tomatoes, blended*
- *1 tsp garlic paste*
- *1 tsp ginger paste*
- *1 medium onion, blended to a mush*
- *1 tsp salt, or to taste*
- *1 ½ tbsp plain yogurt*
- *½ tsp turmeric*
- *50ml water*
- *1 tbsp Kashmiri chilli powder*
- *1 tsp dry coriander powder*
- *1 tomato, finely chopped*
- *3 tbsp sunflower oil*
- *Freshly chopped coriander for garnish*

## METHOD

Firstly, you are going to add ingredients to your pan without turning on the heat. So, take a large wok and add the chopped chicken breast, blended tomatoes, garlic and ginger pastes, mushed onions, salt, yogurt, turmeric, and water.

Place the wok on a high heat and mix all the ingredients well. Keep stirring. Within 6-8 minutes you'll find the chicken is nearly cooked. Add Kashmiri chilli powder and dry coriander. Mix well. Now add the oil and keep stirring. You should be at the point where the chicken is cooked now. Add the chopped tomatoes and chopped coriander. Mix well for a minute and take off the heat.

Serve with chapatis or naan for a super quick curry fix!

# TANDOORI ROAST SPATCHCOCK CHICKEN

You know that your dinner is going to be extra special with this tandoori roasted spatchcock chicken. The yogurt marinade makes the chicken so juicy and tender, and the aromatics will flow through the house as it's cooking.

**SERVES 4**

## INGREDIENTS

- *1 large chicken, spatchcocked (asked your butcher to do this)*

### Marinade Ingredients

- *5 tbsp plain yogurt*
- *3 tbsp sunflower oil*
- *Juice of half a lemon*
- *1 tbsp ginger paste*
- *1 tbsp garlic paste*
- *2 tbsp tandoori powder*
- *1 tbsp green chilli paste*
- *1 tsp garam masala*
- *½ tsp ground black pepper*
- *1 ¼ tsp salt, or to taste*
- *1 tsp red chilli powder*

## METHOD

Score the chicken across the legs, thighs and breast.

Place the chicken in a large, deep baking dish/tray.

Mix together all the marinade ingredients in a bowl and pour over the chicken. Rub it well all around the chicken, especially in the areas where you have scored the chicken.

Cover with aluminium foil and leave to marinate in the fridge overnight. The yogurt in the marinade will tenderise the chicken so it just falls off the bone.

Remove from the fridge an hour before cooking.

Pre-heat the oven to 180 degrees.

Do not remove the aluminium foil from the chicken. Leave as it is, and place in the middle of the oven for 55-60 minutes.

Remove the foil. You will see that there are juices released from the chicken in the base of the tray. Scoop off the juice with a spoon and pour over the chicken. Place back in the oven without the foil for a further 10-15 minutes.

Remove from the oven and let it rest for 10 minutes before serving. Serve with salad, naan and raita and some roast potatoes.

# CHICKEN KEEMA NACHOS

A special twist on nachos as you know it. This could change the way you have nachos forever! My chicken on nachos is just the best! Seriously though, who doesn't love nachos?

**SERVES 4**

## INGREDIENTS

### Ingredients for the keema

- *450g chicken thigh mince*
- *1 onion, finely sliced*
- *2 medium tomatoes*
- *2 tbsp ginger paste*
- *2 tbsp garlic paste*
- *4 green chillies, finely chopped*
- *1 tsp red chilli powder*
- *½ tsp ground black pepper*
- *1 tsp garam masala*
- *1 tsp turmeric*
- *1 tsp coriander powder*
- *1 tsp cumin powder*
- *2 tbsp sunflower oil*
- *1 inch cinnamon stick*
- *2-3 cloves*
- *1 tsp kasuri methi*
- *1 tbsp lemon juice*
- *2 tbsp freshly chopped coriander*

### Nacho Topping Ingredients

- *Lightly salted tortilla chips*
- *3 tbsp mild cheddar, finely grated*
- *1 ripe avocado, roughly chopped*
- *I red onion, finely chopped*
- *1 tomato, finely chopped*
- *2 tbsp pickled jalapenos*
- *Freshly chopped coriander for garnish*
- *150g sour cream dip mixed with 1 tbsp of chilli sauce*

## METHOD

Place a large pan on medium heat with sunflower oil. Add the cloves and cinnamon stick and as they start to sizzle take the pan off the heat and add the ginger paste and garlic paste. Swirl around the oil for 15-20 seconds. Now place back onto the heat along with the sliced onions. Sauté until the onions start to soften. Add the finely chopped green chillies and cook with the onions for a further 2 minutes. Now add the chicken mince. Combine well with the onions and green chillies. Turn the heat down to medium-low and cook for 15 minutes until the mince is nearly cooked through. Add the chopped tomatoes, along with the red chilli powder, garam masala, ground black pepper, turmeric, cumin powder and coriander powder. Simmer for 5 minutes on a low heat, stirring occasionally. Finish off the keema with lemon juice, kasuri methi and chopped coriander. Stir well and take off the heat.

Prepare the nachos in a large serving dish. Evenly spread out the tortilla corn chips across the dish. Top the corn chips with spoonfuls of the chicken keema. Sprinkle over the finely grated cheese. No need to melt the cheese. It is finely grated, so it will slowly melt with the heat from the keema. Scatter over the chopped red onion, tomatoes, pickled jalapenos and avocado. Drizzle with the spicy sour cream sauce, garnish with freshly chopped coriander and serve.

# BUTTER CHICKEN

A rich creamy curry with a silky-smooth texture. The chicken pieces are tender and juicy because of the spiced yogurt marinade. Everyone has their own way of making this curry. Being a family of 4 I like to keep it quick and simple. This is a curry dish that will not disappoint.

**SERVES 4**

## INGREDIENTS

### Ingredients for the chicken marinade

- *500g boneless chicken thigh, cut to 1 inch size pieces*
- *4 tbsp plain yogurt*
- *2 tbsp gram flour*
- *1 tsp coriander powder*
- *1 tsp cumin powder*
- *¼ tsp paprika*
- *1 tbsp Kashmiri chilli powder*
- *1 tsp garam masala*
- *½ tsp lemon juice*
- *1 tsp ginger paste*
- *1 tsp garlic paste*
- *½ tsp green chilli paste*
- *1 tsp salt.*

### Ingredients for gravy

- *2 tbsp sunflower oil*
- *½ inch cinnamon stick*
- *2 green cardamom pods*
- *1 black cardamom pods*
- *4-5 cloves*
- *1 green chilli slit lengthways (I keep the seeds in, but you can deseed)*
- *1 tbsp butter*
- *1 finely chopped onion*
- *4 tsp tomato puree*
- *1 tsp ginger paste*
- *1 tsp garlic paste*
- *1 ½ tsp Kashmiri chilli powder*
- *1 ½ tsp coriander powder*
- *½ tsp turmeric*
- *½ tsp salt*
- *1 tsp honey*
- *250ml double cream*
- *1 tsp kasoori methi*
- *½ tsp garam masala*
- *Chopped coriander for garnish*

## METHOD

Firstly, marinate the chicken in the listed ingredients for the marinade. Leave to marinate in the fridge for 2-4 hours.

Remove the chicken from the fridge an hour before cooking.

Put the chicken on some skewers and grill on a medium-high heat until the edges are charred but the chicken is still moist inside. Approx 20-25 minutes cooking time. Baste and turn the skewers every 10 minutes until cooked.

Now make the butter chicken gravy using the ingredients listed. In a large pan on medium heat, add sunflower oil and butter. To this add cinnamon stick, green and black cardamom pods and cloves. Allow these spices to infuse into the oil and butter. As they start to sizzle add the slit green chilli and then the chopped onions. Cook until slightly browned. Now add the tomato paste. Mix well for a minute. Add ginger and garlic pastes, Kashmiri chilli powder, coriander powder, turmeric, salt and honey. Mix everything together well then add the double cream. Combine all together well. Turn the heat down to low so it simmers nicely. Add kasoori methi and garam masala and stir into the gravy.

Now add the grilled chicken pieces to the gravy and mix well.

Garnish with coriander.

Serve with garlic and coriander naan, plain rice and a salad.

If you have any left over the next day, stir some butter chicken into cooked pasta for a delicious treat for lunch.

# CHICKEN LASOONI (GARLIC CHICKEN)

You could substitute for paneer or tofu using the same process below. A flavour packed, lip smacking Indian curry with a garlic flavoured curry sauce. Every garlic lover's dream! Perfect with naan to scoop up all that gravy

**SERVES 2**

## INGREDIENTS

### Ingredients for the chicken marinade

- *300g boneless Chicken thigh or breast*
- *4 tbsp yogurt*
- *1 tbsp garlic paste*
- *1 tsp chilli powder*
- *½ tsp turmeric*
- *½ tsp garam masala*
- *¼ tsp salt, or to taste*
- *1 tsp kasuri methi (dried fenugreek leaves)*
- *1 tsp lemon juice*
- *1 tbsp sunflower oil*

### Ingredients for the curry paste

- *1 red onion, chopped into small chunks*
- *2 tomatoes, roughly chopped*
- *1 tsp garlic paste*
- *1 tsp ginger paste*
- *15 unsalted cashew nuts*
- *2 tbsp sunflower oil*
- *2 cardamom pods*
- *½ tsp black peppercorns*
- *4 cloves*
- *½ inch piece cinnamon stick*
- *100ml water*

### Remaining ingredients

- *2 tbsp oil*
- *1 tsp ghee*
- *1 small onion, finely chopped*
- *½ tsp cumin seeds*
- *½ tsp turmeric*
- *1 tsp chilli powder*
- *1 tsp ground coriander*
- *½ tsp cumin powder*
- *½ tsp salt, or to taste*
- *½ tsp garam masala*
- *Chopped fresh coriander for garnish*

### For tempering

- *2 tbsp oil*
- *2 cloves of garlic thinly sliced*
- *¼ tsp paprika*
- *1 green chilli finely chopped*

## METHOD

In a mixing bowl, cut the chicken up into inch sized pieces and add all the marinade ingredients. Combine all the ingredients together well with the chicken, or paneer/tofu if you're using an alternative. Place in the fridge and marinate for 2 hours plus. Remember to remove the chicken from the fridge 30 minutes before cooking to bring it to room temperature.

For the curry paste, in a frying pan, heat oil on medium heat and add whole spices – cardamom, black peppercorns, cloves and cinnamon. Let them sizzle for half a minute and then add the chopped red onion. Sauté for a couple of minutes then add the garlic paste and ginger paste. Cook until the onion starts to brown slightly. Now add the chopped tomatoes and cook until they turn soft and mushy. Now add the cashew nuts and stir. Cool this mixture completely and then transfer to a blender with 4 tbsp of water and blend to a smooth curry paste. You can also pre-make the curry paste and leave in the fridge for when you're ready to cook.

Now you can start with the curry base. In a large/wide saucepan, on a medium heat add the oil and ghee. Add the cumin seeds and once they start to sizzle add the finely chopped onion, sauté until they are browned. Now turn the heat down and add all the dry spices – turmeric, chilli powder, ground coriander, cumin powder. Mix all the spices together well and then add the curry paste you made earlier. Add salt and mix well. Put the heat back up to medium and cover the pan with a lid and simmer the curry sauce for around 10 minutes stirring occasionally until you see the oil start to separate at the sides of the curry sauce.

Turn the heat down to low again, take the marinated chicken and add to the curry sauce. The chicken will release its own juices so no need to add water. If you're making this recipe with paneer or tofu add 50ml of water at this point.

Cover and cook until the chicken is tender and cooked through. Add the garam masala and a garnish of coriander. Stir through the curry well. Now the curry is cooked you add some garlic and chilli tempering. In a small saucepan heat the 2 tbsp of oil on a medium heat, add the sliced garlic and brown slightly. Now add the chopped green chilli and paprika. Turn the heat off and swirl all the spices together well in the saucepan. Drizzle over the chicken curry and serve with chapati, naan or rice. Anything to scoop up and soak up all that delicious spicy garlicy sauce.

TIKKA CHICKEN

# TIKKA CHICKEN

Chicken pieces marinated in yogurt and spices. Traditionally cooked on a skewer in a tandoor/clay oven. However, just as delicious cooked in the oven. I don't add any oil to this dish so it's healthy and packed full of flavour. It's quick to cook. The marinade does all the work. The perfect fakeaway. This is one of the first dishes I learned to cook from my mother in law. I've adapted it over the years to suit our ever growing tastebuds.

**SERVES 4**

## INGREDIENTS

- *650g chicken breast*
- *3 tbsp set yogurt*
- *3 tbsp tandoori powder*
- *1 tsp sugar*
- *1 tbsp lemon juice*
- *1 ½ tsp turmeric*
- *1 ½ tsp garam masala*
- *3 tsp green chilli paste*
- *3 tsp garlic paste*
- *1 ½ tsp ginger paste*
- *1 ¼ tsp salt, or to taste*
- *Half red pepper, roughly chopped*
- *Half green pepper, roughly chopped*
- *Chopped fresh coriander for garnish*

## METHOD

Cut the chicken breast into strips, roughly 1 inch wide and 2 inches long, Add to a large mixing bowl along with the set yogurt, tandoori powder, sugar, lemon juice, turmeric, garam masala, green chilli paste, garlic paste, ginger paste and salt. Combine and mix all the spices together well with the chicken. Marinate in the fridge for 2+ hours, preferably overnight to really infuse the chicken with all the spices. When you're ready to cook the chicken, add the chopped red and green peppers to the chicken marinade and stir together with the chicken.

Transfer the marinated chicken and peppers to a large oven proof dish, cover with aluminium foil, pierce the foil several times, and place in a preheated oven at 180 degrees for 30 minutes. After this time, remove the foil and stir the chicken around in all the juices. There will be some water released from the chicken, but the majority of this will evaporate with the remaining time left to cook. Place the dish back into the oven and turn the heat up to 200 degrees. Cook for a further 10 minutes, stirring again halfway.

Garnishing with coriander and serve on a bed of salad or naan with a generous drizzling of raita.

QUICK TAWA CHICKEN

# QUICK TAWA CHICKEN

A popular street food in India.

This is a spicy and succulent quick fix boneless chicken dish that can be prepared in less than 15 minutes. Packed with flavour and spice it will definitely blow your socks off. Traditionally, you would cook this on a tawa (a traditional chapati pan), my OCD won't allow anything other than chapatis on my pan so I use a frying pan. There are so many variations of this dish. This is sizzling and saucy with a kick of spices! Serve with fresh naan and an onion salad!

**SERVES 4**

## INGREDIENTS

- *500g boneless chicken thigh fillets, cut into bitesize chunks*
- *2 finely chopped tomatoes*
- *1 tbsp sunflower oil*
- *1 ½ tsp ginger paste*
- *1 ½ tsp garlic paste*
- *1 ½ tsp red chilli powder*
- *2 chopped green chillies*
- *1 tsp cumin seeds*
- *1 tsp turmeric*
- *1 tsp carom seeds*
- *1 ½ tsp garam masala*
- *2 tsp kasuri methi (dried fenugreek leaves)*
- *3 tsp yogurt*
- *1 tsp salt, or to taste*
- *Chopped fresh coriander for garnish*

## METHOD

Heat a tawa (or a frying pan if you don't have a tawa) on medium heat, add the sunflower oil. Now add the cumin seeds and the carom seeds. Let them sizzle for a few seconds and add the chopped fresh green chillies. Sauté for a few seconds and add the chopped tomatoes. Keep the heat on a medium heat and cook the tomatoes down until they are soft. Now add the ginger and garlic pastes, mix well. Add the turmeric, red chilli powder and garam masala. Now add the chicken thigh pieces and combine well with all the spices. Now add the yogurt and stir through the chicken. Cover with a lid and let it cook for 8-10 minutes stirring often. After 10 minutes remove the lid and you will see the chicken has released its own juices. So now turn the heat up to high and burn off the excess water from the chicken. Keep stirring to make sure you don't burn the chicken. Now add the kasuri methi and stir. Garnish with coriander and serve with some warm garlic and coriander naans and a cucumber kachumber on the side.

# PALAK CHICKEN

Also known as Chicken and Spinach, it's a very popular dish in many Indian restaurants and now you can make your very own at home with this sensational recipe. The spinach marries well with the chicken and the spices infuse into the bitterness of the spinach creating an explosion of flavours and textures. The chicken tastes so tender as the spinach releases water and infuses back into the chicken giving an unbelievable depth of flavour.

Swap the chicken for potato or even paneer for a veggie option.

**SERVES 2-3**

## INGREDIENTS

### Ingredients for the Chicken Marinade

- *500g chicken thigh, cut to your choice of size (I normally cut each thigh into 5-6 chunks)*
- *1 tbsp ginger paste*
- *1 tbsp garlic paste*
- *½ tsp red chilli powder*
- *½ tsp coriander powder*
- *½ tsp cumin powder*
- *½ tsp garam masala*
- *½ tsp salt, or to taste*
- *½ tsp ground black pepper*
- *1 ½ tbsp plain yogurt*
- *1 tsp sunflower oil*

### Ingredients for the palak sauce

- *2-3 tbsp sunflower oil*
- *1 tsp ghee*
- *100g fresh spinach, roughly chopped + 50 ml water*
- *1 ½ medium onions, finely chopped*
- *150g passata + 50ml water*
- *1 tsp ginger paste*
- *1 tsp garlic paste*
- *½ tsp cumin seeds*
- *2 fresh green chillies, chopped*
- *¼ tsp salt, or to taste*
- *½ tsp red chilli powder*
- *½ tsp coriander powder*
- *½ tsp turmeric*
- *1 tsp kasuri methi (dry fenugreek leaves)*
- *½ tsp garam masala*
- *Chopped fresh coriander for garnish*

## METHOD

Marinate the chicken thighs in the ingredients listed and leave to marinate in the fridge for a minimum of 2 hours. When you're ready to cook the chicken, remove from the fridge 30 minutes prior. Heat a wok on a medium-high heat. You don't need to add any oil to the pan because we added that to the chicken marinade. Add the chicken to the wok and flash fry for a couple of minutes. Now turn the heat down and cook the chicken until most of the moisture has evaporated. If the chicken is still slightly undercooked at this point, don't worry because you can finish the cooking off once we add it to the palak sauce.

If you're able to multitask then you can prepare the palak sauce while the chicken is cooking. Don't worry if not. Cook the chicken and set to one side.

In a large/wide saucepan, add the oil and ghee on a medium-low heat. Add the cumin seeds and let them sizzle. Add the finely chopped onions and stir through the oil and cumin seeds. Now add the ginger and garlic pastes and chopped green chillies. Stir well and cook the onions until they are browned, and the oil starts to separate the edges of the onion mixtures. At this point you can add the salt, chilli powder, coriander powder and turmeric. Mix all the spices together well with the onions. Now add the passata and 50ml of water. Cook this for roughly 10-12 minutes on a low heat, stirring occasionally so it doesn't stick to the pan. Again, you should start to see the oil separating at the edges of the mixture. This is good as it means you have incorporated and cooked the spices well with the onions and tomatoes. Now add the chopped spinach and another 50ml of water. Cook for a further 10-12 minutes until you get a beautifully thick palak sauce. Now add the chicken you cooked earlier to the pan. Give it a good mix and simmer with the lid on a low heat for 10 minutes. The chicken and palak should now be well married together with both sets of spices infused together. Add the garam masala and kasuri methi (crushed between the palms of your hands). Give it one last stir and turn off the heat. Give one final flurry of fresh coriander garnish and serve with chapati or pilau rice.

CHICKEN SHAWARMA

# CHICKEN SHAWARMA

Shawarma is another name for sandwich and this one will most definitely knock your socks off! The marination of the chicken is key to this dish and it will drive the simple spice blend to another level. This dish is a certified crowd pleaser and a much healthier option when it comes to satisfying those takeaway cravings.

**SERVES 4**

## INGREDIENTS

- *8 skinless and boneless chicken thighs*
- *Juice and zest of half lemon*
- *1 tbsp olive oil*
- *2 tsp garlic paste*
- *2 tsp smoked paprika*
- *1 tsp ground cumin*
- *1 tsp ground coriander*
- *1 tsp dried chilli flakes*
- *1 tsp sea salt*
- *½ tsp cumin*
- *¼ tsp ground cinnamon*
- *1 tsp cracked black pepper*

## METHOD

In a large airtight container add the chicken, grate in the lemon zest and add the juice of half a lemon. Add the oil, garlic paste and the remaining spices. Mix everything together making well sure the chicken is fully coated. Cover with the lid and marinate in the fridge for at least 2 hours.

Remove the chicken from the fridge around 30 minutes before you're ready to cook. This will allow it to reach room temperature before cooking.

Preheat the oven to 180 degrees. Lightly grease a medium sized loaf tin. Layer the marinated chicken thighs in the loaf tin and press down tightly. Bake for 40-50 minutes in the oven. Check that the chicken is cooked through before removing from the oven. Once cooked let it rest in the tin for 10 minutes or so. Gently tip out of the tin onto a board. Pour any juices left in the tin over the chicken. The chicken will soak it up. Slice the chicken shawarma into slithers and pile onto flatbreads, hummus and salad on the side.

# CHICKEN RASAM

Spicy chicken rasam (soup) to open up those sinuses. It will warm you up from your head to your toes on a cold winter evening! This is my hubby's only request when he's got the 'man flu'. Let me tell you it definitely does the job!

**SERVES 2**

## INGREDIENTS

- *500g chicken (skinned), chopped into 2-3 inch chunks and preferably with bone in*
- *1 tbsp Sunflower oil*
- *½ tsp ghee*
- *2 green cardamom pods*
- *4 black peppercorns*
- *4 cloves*
- *1 bay leaf*
- *1 roughly chopped medium sized onion*
- *1 finely chopped tomato*
- *1 large potato, cut into 8 equal chunks*
- *1200ml of water*
- *1 tsp lemon juice*
- *2 tbsp fresh coriander, chopped + extra for garnish*
- *1 ½ tsp ginger, finely chopped*
- *1 ½ tsp garlic, finely chopped*
- *½ tsp green chilli paste*
- *½ tsp turmeric*
- *½ tsp garam masala*
- *½ tsp red chilli powder*
- *½ tsp salt, or to taste*

## METHOD

In a pressure cooker on medium heat, add the sunflower oil and ghee. Swirl around the pan. Now add the green cardamom pods, peppercorns and cloves. Let them sizzle and become fragrant. Add the chopped onion and sauté until translucent. Add the chopped tomatoes and cook until soft. Now add the chopped ginger and garlic, green chilli paste, turmeric, red chilli powder and salt. Combine everything together well. Add the chopped chicken and potatoes, lemon juice and salt. Stir well to ensure the chicken and potato pieces are coated in all the spices. Add the chopped coriander and 1200ml of water. Put the lid on and pressure cook for 20 minutes. Remove the lid once the steam has completely released naturally from the pressure cooker. Finally add the garam masala and stir through gently. You can keep on a low heat until ready to serve. Garnish with coriander once ready to serve. Serve with warm crusty bread.

CHICKEN BALTI FILO PIE

# CHICKEN BALTI FILO PIE

Curry in a pie! Oh yes you heard me right, my family cannot have a meal without at least a bit of spice! The fiery fiasco of a chicken Balti wrapped in a flaky filo pastry case. You don't need to serve this with anything as the pie is packed with so many rich flavours it goes without saying that pie lovers will go crazy over this dish!

Make it with left over curry, the matured taste makes this pie even more sensational than you can imagine!

**SERVES 4-6**

## INGREDIENTS

### Ingredients for the marinade

- *900g chicken breasts, cut into small bitesize chunks*
- *1 ½ green peppers, roughly chopped*
- *3 tsp garlic paste*
- *3 tsp ginger paste*
- *1 tsp garam masala*
- *1 tsp cumin seeds*
- *1 tsp salt, or to taste*
- *2 tsp paprika*
- *4 tbsp plain set yogurt*
- *Juice from half a lemon*

### Ingredients for the Tikka sauce

- *3 tbsp sunflower oil*
- *2 medium onions, finely chopped*
- *2 tbsp garlic paste*
- *2 tbsp ginger paste*
- *2 tsp red chilli powder*
- *¼ tsp ground cinnamon*
- *1 ½ tsp turmeric*
- *2 tsp dry coriander powder*
- *2 tsp ground cumin*
- *1 ½ tsp garam masala*
- *1 tsp smoked paprika*
- *½ tsp honey*
- *1 tsp salt, or to taste*
- *2 tsp double concentrated tomato puree*
- *1 tin chopped tomatoes 400g*
- *100ml of single cream*
- *30g freshly coriander finely chopped.*

### Other ingredients

- *1 packet of pre-rolled filo pastry sheets*
- *Oil for greasing*
- *Oil to brush the filo*
- *Nigella and Sesame seeds to scatter over the filo*

## METHOD

In a mixing bowl, add the chicken, the chopped green peppers and mix together with all the ingredients listed for the marinade. Make sure the chicken and peppers are fully coated in all the spices and yogurt. Transfer to an airtight container and marinate for 2 hours plus. I normally do this process the night before to give plenty of time for the spices to infuse into the chicken.

Once marinated, give the chicken another mix before transferring to a baking/roasting dish. Spread evenly around the dish and grill on a medium heat for 20-25 minutes turning half way.

While the chicken and peppers are grilling away nicely you can start to prepare the tikka sauce. In a wide saucepan heat the oil on a medium heat, add the onions and sauté until slightly browned. Now add the garlic and ginger pastes, stir through the onions. Add the remaining ground spices – red chilli powder, turmeric, garam masala, paprika, ground cinnamon, coriander and cumin. Mix all the spices until combined and cook for a few minutes stirring occasionally until they release a beautiful aroma. Now add the tomato puree paste and cook for a further 2 minutes. Add the tinned tomatoes, salt, and sugar. As it starts to bubble away, turn the heat down to low and simmer.

Back to the chicken under the grill, it should be sitting slightly charred in all the juices from the chicken and the spices. Add the grilled chicken and pepper along with all its juices into the tikka sauce that is simmering away. Turn the heat right up to high, stirring often, cook until all the water and juices have evaporated, the sauce has thickened, and you're left with a semi-saucy chicken Balti curry. This should take about 5-6 minutes. Add the cream and fresh coriander and stir through the chicken balti. Take off the heat and set to one side.

Now preheat the oven to 200 degrees celsius.

Place the filo pastry under a damp cloth to prevent it from drying out.

Grease an 18-inch round pie dish, or use a spring form tin, if so it's easier to remove the pie from the tin.

Take one sheet of the filo pastry and brush with the oil and place oil side down in the dish/tin so the pastry is overlapping the outside of the dish. Continue to brush all the sheets one by one with oil and lay into the dish creating a secure and gap free casing for the chicken balti mixture. Once you have 1 layer repeat until you built up 4 layers of filo.

Now spoon all the chicken balti mixture into the filo casing. Spread the chicken out evenly and cover with the overlapping filo sheets. Brush the top of the pie with some more oil. This will make the pastry golden and crispy. Sprinkle nigella seeds over it. Place the dish the middle of the oven and bake until the pastry is cooked and golden in colour. All that's left to do is slice and serve. Tastes absolutely divine with mint and coriander raita and my cumin potato shaak *(page 93)* on the side. A hearty and satisfying meal.

# MEAT

# MASALA LAMB SHANK

This is a hearty dish packed with flavour from the marinade. The shanks are slow cooked until tender in a delicious masala gravy seasoned with beautiful earthy aromatics. Perfect for a special dinner party or a weekend treat. The gravy oozes depth with warming flavours and the meat just falls off the bone. (My husband loves this one).

**SERVES 4**

## INGREDIENTS

### Ingredients for the marinade

- *4 lamb shanks*
- *7 tbsp natural yogurt*
- *2 tsp lemon juice*
- *1 tsp salt*

### Other ingredients

- *4 tbsp sunflower oil*
- *3 onions, finely chopped*
- *1 ½ tbsp ginger paste*
- *1 ½ tbsp garlic paste*
- *6 ripe tomatoes, finely chopped*
- *3 tsp red chilli powder*
- *½ tsp turmeric*
- *3 tsp coriander powder*
- *3 tsp cumin powder*
- *2 tsp garam masala*
- *2 ½ tsp kasuri methi (dried fenugreek)*
- *1 ½ tsp salt, or to taste*
- *1 tsp ground black pepper*
- *4 tsp tomato puree*
- *4 black cardamom*
- *5 green cardamom*
- *1 inch piece cinnamon stick*
- *2 bay leaves*
- *400ml water*
- *Freshly chopped coriander for garnish*
- *Freshly chopped mint for garnish*
- *Pomegranate seeds for garnish*
- *Flaked almond for garnish*

## METHOD

To begin make the yogurt, lemon and salt marinade in a bowl and set aside. Clean and wash the shanks, trimming off any excess fat. Create inch incisions. Rub the lamb shanks with the marinade. Marinate in the fridge for a minimum of 2 hours. Remove from the fridge 30 minutes before cooking to bring to room temperature.

Place a large, deep oven proof casserole dish, on medium heat. Heat the sunflower oil and add the chopped onions. Fry the onions until they become just slightly browned. Add the cinnamon stick, bay leaves, green cardamom and black cardamom. Stir well with the onions and cook until the onions are fully browned and caramelised. Add a splash of water if you feel the onions are sticking to the bottom of the pan. Now add the ginger paste and garlic paste and sauté with the onions for a further 2 minutes.

Now add the chopped tomatoes and stir through with the cooked onions. Cook for a few minutes until the tomatoes start to soften. Now add red chilli powder, turmeric, cumin powder, coriander powder, salt and ground black pepper. Mix and combine all the spices well with the onion and tomato mix. Cook for 10 minutes. Again, add a few splashes of water if you feel the mixture is sticking or becoming dry. The masala base is now ready.

After the 10 minutes have passed, add the marinated lamb shanks. Turn the heat up to high and seal all sides of the shanks. The yogurt from the shanks will help form part of the sauce base with the masala base. Once the shanks are sealed on all sides, turn the heat down to low and add 400ml of water. Stir gently.

Now place the lid on the dish and continue to slow cook in the oven at 160 degrees for 3 hours, stirring occasionally during this time. Add water if required to keep a thick gravy consistency.

Halfway through the cooking time, add the tomato puree, garam masala and kasuri methi. Stir gently. Cover and cook for the remaining time.

Serve on a bed of rice and garnish with freshly chopped coriander and mint, pomegranate seeds and flaked almonds.

This lamb will not only be rich and aromatic but will fall off the bone tender and succulent.

LAMB KEEMA

# LAMB KEEMA

A traditionally spiced curry with all the usual culprits of a spicy curry. A dish packed full of spices and aroma. I always add a larger quantity of spices when it comes to lamb as it really compliments the warming richness of lamb meat. I like to make extra portions so we can make keema cheese wraps with the left overs.

# LAMB KEEMA

**SERVES 4**

## INGREDIENTS

- *500g lean lamb mince*
- *2 medium onions, finely chopped*
- *2 medium potatoes, each one cut into 6 equal chunks*
- *2 cinnamon sticks*
- *2 green cardamom pods*
- *4 cloves*
- *1 bay leaf*
- *5 tbsp sunflower oil*
- *1 tsp ghee*
- *1 tsp green chilli paste*
- *1 ½ tsp ginger paste*
- *1 ½ tsp garlic paste*
- *1 tsp tomato paste*
- *1 tsp red chilli powder*
- *1 tsp turmeric*
- *1 ½ tsp dry coriander powder*
- *1 ½ tsp cumin powder*
- *1 ½ tsp salt, or to taste*
- *400g tin tomatoes, blended*
- *1 tsp garam masala*
- *1 tbsp kasuri methi*
- *1 tbsp chopped fresh spring garlic (optional)*
- *2 tbsp chopped fresh coriander*
- *a handful of garden peas*

## METHOD

In a heavy bottom pan, heat the oil on medium-low heat. Add the ghee and swirl around in the oil until melted. Add the cinnamon sticks, green cardamom pods, cloves and bay leaf. Let them sizzle and become fragrant. Now add the finely chopped onions and reduce the heat to low. Cook the onions until they are browned. Now add the garlic, ginger, green chilli pastes and tomato paste. Stir and cook for a few minutes. Now add the lamb mince and stir well with onion mixture. Cook the meat with the lid on for around 10 minutes, stirring occasionally, until it has browned. You will find there will be juices released from the meat. This is good as it helps create a sauce without adding any extra water. Now add the red chilli powder, turmeric, dry coriander powder, cumin powder and salt. Stir all the spices together well with the meat and cook for a few more minutes. Now add the blended tinned tomatoes and combine well with everything. Add the potatoes. Close the lid and cook on low for 30 minutes, stirring occasionally until the potatoes are cooked through. Add the garam masala and kasuri methi. If you grow your own spring garlic, fantastic! If not, you may be able to locally source some. Garnish the keema at the end with the spring garlic and coriander. It just takes it to the next level.

Serve with chapati or naan and onions.

# MASALA LAMB CHOPS

My juicy tender lamb chops are a complete delight. They are warming, aromatic, succulent and flavourful. Coated in a masala paste and cooked low and slow. If you're stuck for time you can griddle these quicker. They will be just as tasty.

**SERVES 4**

## INGREDIENTS

- *12 Chops (back chops preferably)*
- *2 tsp green chilli paste*
- *2 tsp garlic paste*
- *½ tsp ginger paste*
- *2 tsp salt, or to taste*
- *1 tsp red chilli powder*
- *1 tsp turmeric*
- *2 tsp garam masala*
- *2 tsp tomato puree*
- *4 tsp kasuri methi (dried fenugreek leaves)*
- *1 tbsp sunflower oil*
- *½ tsp lemon juice*
- *3 tbsp fresh coriander, finely chopped*
- *Lime wedges, for garnish*

## METHOD

Marinate the lamb chops in all the listed ingredients. Place the marinated chops in the fridge to marinate for 2+ hours, or overnight if possible.

Remove the marinated chops from the fridge 20 minutes before cooking.

Place the chops in a deep oven proof dish and cover with aluminium foil. Place it on the middle shelf of a preheated oven at 150 degrees for 1 hour 30 minutes. Remove the foil, basting the chops in the surrounding juices and place back in the oven on the top shelf without the foil for a further 30 minutes.

Once cooked, let the chops rest for 15 minutes before serving. They will be so tender and juicy. Literally they will be falling apart.

Enjoy with a squeeze of lime and a raita on the side.

These are also fantastic on the bbq, or equally delicious cooked in a griddle pan on the stove, for a quicker cooking process.

*Masala marinade for the lamb chops*

# LAMB GOSHT

This is a slow cooked lamb curry which I learned to cook after I got married. There are many variations to this curry as I have seen several recipes vastly different to mine. I've learned and adapted and enhanced my way of cooking this particular curry over the last few years. Perfection does not happen overnight although, after many trials and errors I finally cracked it. Lamb Gosht is a curry very close to my husband's family and their traditions. Even my mother in law has a completely different recipe to me. My husband has memories of this being eaten at special occasions such as weddings and other special celebrations. That's because it's a very rich, dark dish made with the most succulent and tender morsels of lamb meat and soft floury potatoes, packed with spices, aromatics and the essence of fulfilment. The thick gravy brings a heart-warming delight to every mouthful. The spices in this curry marry with the slight sweetness of the rich tomato gravy. It's utterly hard to resist. This is definitely a curry for a special occasion or when you have family and friends over. I can guarantee it will be an absolute hit every single time.

**SERVES 4**

## INGREDIENTS

- *2 lb lamb shoulder meat with bone*
- *3 medium white onions, finely diced*
- *1 tin chopped/plum tomatoes (400g), blended to a liquid*
- *1 small aubergine, finely chopped*
- *6-8 tbsp sunflower oil*
- *2 cinnamon sticks*
- *6-8 cloves*
- *1 tsp finely chopped ginger*
- *1 tsp finely chopped garlic*
- *1 tbsp tomato puree*
- *2 tsp ginger paste.*
- *2 tsp garlic paste*
- *2 tsp turmeric*
- *3 tsp red chilli powder*
- *2 tsp salt, or to taste*
- *2 tsp dry ground coriander*
- *2 tsp ground cumin*
- *2 tsp garam masala*
- *300ml of water*
- *8 baby potatoes, peeled*
- *Chopped fresh coriander for garnish*
- *pomegranate seeds for garnish*

## METHOD

Wash the meat under the tap with warm water. Drain any excess water in a colander.

I like to use a large, heavy copper pan when cooking lamb gosht. Not only do they transmit heat quickly and evenly, they also retain the heat for hours after cooking, making the lamb even more succulent after the cooking process has finished.

On a medium heat, add oil to the pan along with the cinnamon and cloves. Wait for them to sizzle. Then I turn the heat off and add the chopped ginger and garlic and swirl around in the oil. The reason I turn the heat off at this point is because I don't want to burn the ginger and garlic, I want to flavour the oil with aromatics of the ginger and garlic. Now turn the heat back on and add the meat. The oil should still be hot so you will hear the meat sizzle as it hits the pan. Give it a good stir, turn the heat down to low and put the lid on for a few minutes. Next, evenly spread the meat out in the bottom on the pan. Now note from this point on you will not stir the meat until at least an hour of cooking time has passed. You've spread the meat around the pan so now you firstly add the onions on top of the meat, then the diced aubergine, ginger and garlic pastes, turmeric, red chilli powder, salt, ground coriander and ground cumin. Top with the blended tin of tomatoes and 450ml of water. Remember do not stir any of the ingredients. That's the beauty of my gosht recipe. You add everything all together in the pan and let the cooking do its magic! Put the lid back on the pan, keep on a low heat and continue to simmer for an hour and a half. After an hour of cooking time has passed lift the lid and give it a gentle stir to ensure it's not sticking to the bottom of the pan. Place the lid back and continue cooking for the remaining half hour. After this time has passed, lift the lid to stir gently. The gosht will be bubbling away nicely with the tender pieces of lamb in a rich, deep red coloured gravy. At this point you can add the peeled baby potatoes, tomato puree and garam masala. Push the potatoes right into the pan between all the meat pieces to ensure they cook through. Replace the lid for a further 15 minutes or so, until the potatoes are just cooked through. You don't want them over cooking otherwise they will start to crumble and break away in the gravy. By now the meat will be so tender and juicy, literally falling off the bone as you gently swirl the curry around the pan. The fragrant aromas of the spices will be incredibly mind blowing. Turn off the heat and replace the lid to retain the heat. When you are ready to serve, garnish with coriander and slivers of ginger. Serve with white rice, pickled red onions and a cooling yogurt.

# MINI LAMB KEBAB TIKKIS

My lamb kebabs tikkis are to die for, trust me! They are crowd-friendly, kid-friendly and you can freeze ahead, so they are super convenient. Warmly spiced with garam masala, fragrant with onion, ginger and garlic, and so tender and juicy. We like to eat these rolled up in some naan with my simple kachumbar salad and mint sauce. This recipe makes quite a few kebabs so it's a good opportunity to stash some away in the freezer for another meal. Therefore, it beats a takeaway any day!

**SERVES 4**

## INGREDIENTS

### Ingredients for the lamb marinade

- *500g lean mince lamb*
- *1 finely chopped yellow onion*
- *½ tsp green chilli paste*
- *½ tsp ginger paste*
- *1 tsp garlic paste*
- *1 tsp dry ground coriander*
- *1 tsp ground cumin*
- *½ tsp ground dried mint*
- *1 tsp salt, or to taste*
- *½ tsp whole cumin seeds*
- *1 ½ tsp red chilli powder*
- *½ tsp garam masala*

### Other ingredients

- *2 tbsp sunflower oil*
- *1 cinnamon stick*
- *3-4 cloves*

## METHOD

Marinate the mince lamb (keema) in all the ingredients listed. I'd suggest wearing some disposable gloves and really getting your hands in there to combine all the spices together with the mince. Marinate in the fridge for a minimum of 2 hours. If you have the time to prepare this the night before then it is even better to allow additional time for the spices to really infuse the lamb.

Remove from the fridge half an hour before cooking. Grease your hand with some oil to prevent the keema sticking to your hands. Divide the keema into approx. 30 equal sized round balls. Now flatten each one ever so slightly with the palm of your hands and set to one side.

Heat a large frying pan on medium heat with sunflower oil, cinnamon and cloves. Listen for that sizzle of the whole spices and for that pleasing aroma to be released. Add the prepared kebabs to the pan. Depending on the size of your frying pan, you may need to cook in smaller batches. Cook the kebabs on one side and you will notice roughly after 10 minutes they will have started to brown. You may want to use a splatter guard over the frying pan, as the kebabs tend to spit back you. Once they start to brown on one side, flip over the kebabs to cook on the other side. By now they will have started to release their own oils and juices. Cook for a further 10 minutes on the other side, or until they have evenly browned and cooked through. Avoid cooking on a high flame as this will cause them to burn on the outside and they will remain uncooked on the inside.

Serve with my homemade naan *(page 161)*, kachumbar salad and mint sauce. Fake-away at its finest!

You can also use this recipe to turn the marinated mince into lamb burgers. Add some grated cheese to the mince and bind together to form burger patties. Cook on a griddle or on the bbq, then sandwich in a brioche bun with some raita and salad.

LAMB KOFTA CURRY

# LAMB KOFTA CURRY

This is a super easy curry made with my lamb kebab tikki recipe. This is a flexible dish that can be eaten with a variety of things. Other than the usual rice or naan, we also love to eat this with spaghetti, aka, spaghetti and meatballs. The flavoured meat takes Indian fusion to a whole new level!

**SERVES 4**

## INGREDIENT

### Ingredients for the meatballs

- *Marinate 500g mince lamb as per my lamb kebab tikki recipe. Once marinated roll into equal sized kofta balls, around the width of a 2p coin*

### Ingredients for the curry base

- *4 tbsp sunflower oil*
- *1 cinnamon stick*
- *2 bay leaves*
- *½ tsp cumin seeds*
- *3 large white onions, finely chopped*
- *2 tbsp garlic paste*
- *2 tbsp ginger paste*
- *1 tsp green chilli paste*
- *550g passata*
- *2 tsp ground coriander*
- *1 tsp ground cumin*
- *1 tsp turmeric*
- *1 tsp red chilli powder*
- *1 ½ tsp salt*
- *2 tsp tomato puree*
- *600ml of warm water*
- *1 ½ tbsp kasuri methi*
- *1 tsp garam masala*
- *Chopped fresh coriander for garnish*

## METHOD

In a heavy bottom frying pan heat the sunflower oil on medium heat, add the cinnamon stick, bay leaves and cumin seeds. Let them sizzle for a couple of minutes before adding the finely chopped onions. Brown the onions on a low heat. Once the onions are a golden colour add the garlic paste, ginger paste and green chilli paste. Cook the spices on a low heat for a few minutes before adding the red chilli powder, ground coriander, ground cumin, turmeric, salt and tomato puree. Mix all the spices together well with the onions. Now add the Passata. Mix well and cook all the spices with the passata for 8-10 minutes on a low heat until the oil separates at the edges. Now add 600ml warm water, stir and gently bring to boil on a medium heat. Add the lamb kofta balls and continue to simmer on medium heat for 10 minutes. Now the meatball curry should be bubbling away nicely. Crush the kasuri methi between the palms of your hands and add to the curry. Also add half a tsp of the garam masala now. Stir gently and place the lid on the pan and simmer on a low heat for a further 1 hour, stirring occasionally. Finish with ½ tsp of garam masala and a generous scattering of fresh coriander.

Pour over spaghetti for a deliciously hearty meal, or enjoy simply with some chapati, naan or rice.

KEEMA AND CHORIZO LASAGNE

# KEEMA AND CHORIZO LASAGNE

This is my Indian inspired lasagne. Anyone who's eaten my lasagne instantly wants the recipe as it is a proper hearty and filling meal. This recipe combines the best of both worlds for me. The Indian spices and flavours come together so beautifully with the pasta sheets and cheeses. Loaded with cheese, there are no low-fat shortcuts here. This is not your typical lasagne, although, it is comfort food at its finest therefore, prepare to be wowed! This recipe might look long, but it's actually pretty simple. I've broken the ingredients down into 3 parts making it easy for you to put together this lasagne.

**SERVES 4-6**

## INGREDIENTS

### Ingredients for the red Bolognese sauce:

- *1 tin chopped tomatoes, 400g*
- *1 tbsp minced garlic*
- *2 tsp Italian herbs (dried)*
- *1 tsp salt, or to taste*
- *1 ½ tsp sugar*
- *1/2 tsp ground black pepper*
- *2 tsp olive oil*

### Ingredients for the cheese sauce

- *1 tbsp salted butter*
- *1 tbsp plain flour*
- *250ml of pasteurised milk*
- *1 tsp olive oil*
- *1 tsp salt, or to taste*
- *1 tsp white pepper*
- *100g strong mature cheddar*

### Other ingredients

- *1 lb lean mince lamb*
- *1 yellow onion, diced*
- *2 carrots, diced into small chunks*
- *Half a floret of broccoli (separating the florets into easy to eat morsels)*
- *100g of diced spicy Spanish chorizo - pan fried.*
- *2 tbsp olive oil*
- *½ tsp fennel seeds*
- *1 tsp minced garlic*
- *1 tsp red chilli flakes*
- *1 tsp coarse black pepper*
- *½ tsp salt, or to taste*
- *½ tsp garam masala*
- *25g grated parmesan*
- *200g mild cheddar*
- *100g mozzarella ball*
- *Pack or fresh lasagne sheets (normally there are 6 sheets in a packet)*

# KEEMA AND CHORIZO LASAGNE

## METHOD

Firstly, you can make the Bolognese sauce and cheese sauce and set them to one side. For the Bolognese sauce, heat the oil in a saucepan, add the garlic and sauté for a minute. Add the tinned tomatoes along with the dried herbs, sugar, salt and pepper. Simmer for 15-20 minutes on a medium to low heat until the tomatoes start to break down and sauce thickens slightly. Put this to one side and start on the cheese sauce.

Heat oil and butter in a saucepan. Add the flour and roast it until you get a nice aroma and it turns a golden colour. Slowly pour in the milk and whisk continuously to break down any lumps of flour. Bring to boil. As soon as the mixture starts to thicken reduce the heat and add the cheese, salt and pepper and stir. Take off the heat and put to one side along with the Bolognese sauce.

Now you can start to prepare and cook the lasagne filling. In a large wok or pan, on a medium to low heat, add the oil and the fennel seeds until they start to sizzle. Now throw in the chopped onions and sauté until softened and translucent. Add the lamb mince and stir thoroughly with the onions. Cook until the lamb starts to brown slightly. Now add the chopped carrots and broccoli, garlic paste, red chilli flakes, black pepper, salt and garam masala. Mix well making sure all the spices are combined well within the lamb. Now add the Bolognese sauce you prepared earlier. Stir into the lamb and simmer for 15 minutes. In the meantime dry fry the chorizo in a frying pan. It will release it's own oil, so no need to add any extra. Cook until they are golden and crisp. Add the chorizo and all the oils and juices to the lamb that's simmering away. Sprinkle in the parmesan cheese, gently stir and turn off the heat. The Keema filling is now ready.

You can make all the above in advance and layer the lasagne when you are ready to eat.

Preheat the oven at 180 degrees.

I normally use a 11 x 8 approx. lasagne dish. I like to brush the bottom of the dish with some of the lasagne filling to avoid the lasagne sheets sticking. Place the first layer of lasagne sheets at the bottom of the dish. You may need to cut the sheets to a size that fits your dish. I like to make just a 2 layered thick lasagne, but you feel free to make as many layers as you like. If you want to make it my way, split the lamb keema into 2 equal portions. Add the first portion on top of the layered lasagne sheets in the dish. Make sure it's spread out evenly. Now a thin layer of the cheese sauce on top of this (if the cheese sauce has thickened to much, heat it up again to loosen the sauce) sprinkle a handful of the grated cheddar on top of the cheese sauce layer. Now add another layer of the lasagne sheets, then the remaining lamb keema, then some more cheese sauce and another scattering of grated cheddar. Now layer the top of the lasagne with the last layer of lasagne sheets. Cover the top of the sheets with the cheese sauce, and a generous scattering of grated cheddar. Tear the mozzarella ball up into bitesize chunks and place each piece spaced out on top of the cheddar. It might sound like cheese overload but trust me you will be in heaven with the first mouthful.

Place the lasagne dish in the oven for approx. 35-40 minutes, until the cheddar cheese is bubbling, and the mozzarella has started to crisp on top.

This is quite the hearty dish, so it doesn't need any heavy accompaniments. A simple rocket salad goes perfectly with this incredibly delicious meal. Enjoy!

# SPICED SCOTCH EGGS

I love a scotch egg. The joy that my spiced scotch eggs bring is pure satisfaction. Perfect to make ahead of time for a picnic or outing. The golden crumb is a beautiful contrast with the spices in the pork filling. These will become a real versatile favourite.

**SERVES 4**

## INGREDIENTS

- *4 large eggs + 1 egg for coating*
- *8 good quality pork sausages, casing removed, so you have just the sausage meat*
- *2 tsp garlic paste*
- *½ tsp turmeric*
- *½ tsp chilli powder*
- *2 tsp red chilli flakes*
- *½ tsp cumin powder*
- *½ tsp coriander powder*
- *1 tbsp freshly chopped parsley*
- *1 tbsp freshly chopped coriander*
- *½ tsp salt*
- *½ tsp ground black pepper*
- *Plain flour for dusting*
- *200g of breadcrumbs*
- *Sunflower oil for deep frying*

## METHOD

Fill a medium sized saucepan with water and bring to boil. Slowly place the eggs into the pan and simmer for 6 minutes. Remove the eggs and place in a bowl of cold water to stop them cooking. Once the eggs have completely cooled, peel the shell and leave eggs to one side.

In a large mixing bowl add the sausage meat along with the garlic paste, turmeric, chilli powder, chilli flakes, cumin powder, coriander powder, salt, pepper, parsley and coriander. Mix and combine all the ingredients together well.

Divide the sausage mixture up into 4 equal balls.

Using cling film, flatten one of the balls of meat in between the film using your palms, creating a thin even patty.

Lightly dust one of the eggs with plain flour.

Remove the top layer of the cling film from the sausage patty and place the floured egg in the middle of the patty. Lift the sausage patty and egg with the cling film still underneath and wrap the sausage meat around the egg with the help of the cling film. Make sure the egg is completely covered with the sausage meat. At this point you can remove the cling film.

Repeat this process with the remaining 3 eggs and sausage meat.

Now to coat the sausage-eggs. Put some flour on 1 plate, and breadcrumbs on another. Whisk an egg in a bowl.

Now roll the sausage-eggs in the flour. Then dip evenly in the beaten egg. Finally roll the ball in the breadcrumbs, covering the ball evenly all around. Repeat the process for the remaining sausage-eggs.

Heat the sunflower oil in a large pan to 160 degrees. Carefully lower the scotch eggs into the oil. Fry 2 at a time. Turning often, fry for approx. 10 minutes until the outer coating turns crispy and golden.

Once cooked, transfer to kitchen paper to drain excess oil.

Serve with a salad and raita.

# FISH

# CREAMY SALMON MAKHANI

This is a delicious amalgamation of perfectly fried salmon fillets with a creamy, rich, buttery makhani gravy that will tantalize your tastebuds and make you crave more. It is a mouth-watering recipe that is popular with my whole family, even the little ones.

**SERVES 4-6**

## INGREDIENTS

### Ingredients to marinate the salmon -

- *6 salmon fillets, cut into approx 2 inch chunks*
- *3 tbsp sunflower oil + 2 tbsp for cooking the salmon*
- *1 tsp garlic paste*
- *Juice of ½ lemon*
- *½ tsp salt*
- *1 tsp Kashmiri chilli powder*
- *½ tsp turmeric*
- *½ tsp garam masala*
- *½ tsp brown sugar*

### Ingredients for the Makhani sauce

- *2 tbsp sunflower oil*
- *1 tbsp butter*
- *1 tsp garlic paste*
- *½ tsp ginger paste*
- *1-2 green chillies slit down the middle*
- *400g tin of tomatoes, blended*
- *1 tsp dry coriander*
- *1 tsp cumin powder*
- *1 tsp Kashmiri chilli powder*
- *1 tsp turmeric*
- *1 tsp salt*
- *300ml single cream*
- *2 tsp crushed kasuri methi*
- *½ tsp garam masala*
- *Freshly chopped coriander for garnish*

## METHOD

Firstly marinate the salmon fillets with the ingredients listed, cover and marinate for at least 2 hours.

To make the makhani sauce, heat sunflower oil in a pan on low heat with the butter. Add the ginger and garlic pastes and the green chillies. Swirl through the oil and butter and cook on a low heat for a few minutes. Add the blended tinned tomatoes along with the dry coriander, cumin powder, Kashmiri chilli powder, turmeric and salt. Mix and combine well. Continue to cook on a medium to low heat until you see the oil separate from the tomato mix. Reduce the heat to low. At this point add the single cream and stir through gently. Add the crushed kasuri methi and garam masala. Stir through the makhani sauce and take off the heat.

Now to pan fry the salmon. Heat 2 tbsp of sunflower oil in a frying pan on medium to high heat. Place the salmon chunks skin side down into the frying pan and turn the heat down to medium. Continue to fry skin side down for 5 minutes, then flip the fillet chunks over and fry for a further 2-3 minutes.

Add the cooked salmon chunks to the delicious creamy makhani sauce and gently incorporate with the sauce. Garnish with freshly chopped coriander and serve immediately with naan and jeera rice.

CHILLI GARLIC PRAWN PURI

# CHILLI GARLIC PRAWN PURI

Hot and spicy prawns with light fluffy puris is a match made in heaven. I love the combination of spiciness with the sweetness of the prawns all wrapped up in a puri blanket. Simply divine and so simple as a quick dish to whip up and takes even less time to gobble up!

**SERVES 2**

## INGREDIENTS

- *2 tbsp sunflower oil*
- *1 tsp butter*
- *2 tbsp finely chopped garlic*
- *2 shallots, finely chopped*
- *200g raw king prawns*
- *2 tsp red chilli flakes*
- *½ tsp salt, or to taste*
- *1 tsp ground black pepper*
- *1 tsp paprika*
- *1 tsp lemon juice*
- *3 tbsp finely chopped spring onions*
- *Finely chopped coriander for garnish*

### Puri Ingredients

Same recipe *(page 155)* but double up the size of the dough balls.

## METHOD

In a large wok on high heat, add the sunflower oil and butter. Swirl around until the butter has melted. Add the chopped garlic and sauté for a minute on a medium heat. Now add finely chopped shallots. Toss around the pan for a minute. Add the prawns and stir fry with the garlic for a minute before adding the red chilli flakes, salt, black pepper and paprika. Turn the heat up high and cook stirring/tossing often for 2 minutes. Now add the lemon juice and stir. Turn the heat down to low as the prawns will be cooked now. Add the chopped spring onion and toss everything together well. Garnish with coriander and serve on top of your fried puri with salad and raita.

# INDIAN SPICED FISH 'N' CHIPS WITH MASALA MUSHY PEAS

Friday isn't Friday without good old fish 'n' chips (that's the British in me). So well deserved after a hectic week. My Indian adaptation of a British classic enhances the flavours so you will not be disappointed.

**SERVES 4**

## INGREDIENTS

### Ingredients for the fish marinade

- *4 boneless white fish fillets (can use frozen – just defrost before use)*
- *1 tsp garlic paste*
- *1 tsp ginger paste*
- *½ tsp coriander powder*
- *½ tsp red chilli powder*

### Ingredients for the fish batter

- *½ tsp turmeric*
- *½ tsp ground white pepper*
- *¾ tsp salt, or to taste*
- *1 ½ tbsp cornflour + extra for dusting*
- *Pinch of baking powder*
- *4 tbsp plain flour*
- *3 tsp rice flour*
- *100ml soda water, use cold from the fridge*
- *Vegetable oil for deep frying*

### Ingredients for the chips

- *4 large maris piper potatoes, peeled and cut into chunky chips*
- *4 tbsp oil*
- *½ tsp salt, or to taste*
- *½ tsp black pepper powder*
- *½ tsp red chilli powder*
- *Pinch of turmeric*

### Ingredients for mushy peas

- *300g tin marrowfat peas*
- *1 red onion, finely chopped*
- *1 red chilli, finely chopped*
- *1 tsp finely chopped fresh mint*
- *½ tsp cumin powder*
- *½ coriander powder*
- *Pinch of garam masala*
- *5 garlic cloves, finely chopped*
- *2 tbsp butter*
- *1 tbsp sunflower oil*

## METHOD

Defrost the fish and pat dry to soak up any excess moisture.

Marinate the fish in the ginger paste, garlic paste, coriander powder and red chilli powder. Leave to marinate whilst you prepare the chips.

Place your peeled and cut chips into a pan of water and parboil for 10 mins until they start to just soften and still holding their shape. Drain the water and gently pat dry the potatoes.

Transfer the potatoes to a baking tray, coat them in the oil and place into the oven at 200 degrees for 30 minutes, turning the chips halfway. Mix the remaining ingredients for the chips in a bowl to make the seasoning (salt, black pepper, turmeric and red chilli powder). Set to one side.

Now for the mushy peas, heat oil in a saucepan on a medium heat and add the butter. Once the butter has melted into the oil, add the finely chopped onion and sauté until translucent. Now add the finely chopped garlic cloves. Sauté with the onions for a couple of minutes. Turn the heat down to low and stir in the cumin powder, coriander powder, salt, black pepper and garam masala. Cook the spices with the onions for a minute before adding the marrowfat peas. Sauté for 2-3 minutes on a low heat. Mash the peas gently leaving some chunks for texture. Add some splashes of water if necessary. Garnish with the finely chopped chilli and chopped mint. Place to the side for later.

Prepare the batter for the fish by sifting together in a bowl the cornflour, plain flour, rice flour and baking powder. To which add turmeric, ground white pepper and salt. Mix well. Gradually add the cold soda water and whisk until you have a smooth, runny batter.

To fry the fish, heat oil in a deep-frying pan to 190 degrees.

Lightly dust each of your marinated fish fillets in cornflour. This will help the batter to stick to the fish.

Now dip each lightly dusted fish fillet into the masala batter, let the excess drip off and carefully place into your hot oil. Don't overcrowd the pan with all the fillets otherwise it will result in a drop in the oil temperature.

Fry for 3-4 minutes on each side until golden and crispy on both sides. Place the fried fish on a wire rack to drain any excess oil.

Finally, take your chips out of the oven, evenly coat the chips in the seasoning mix you made earlier and place back in the oven for a further 5-8 minutes.

Plate up your crispy fish, with your masala chips, mushy peas and a wedge of lemon.

TANDOORI PRAWNS

# TANDOORI PRAWNS

These easy to make prawns are spicy, juicy, smoky and sensationally succulent. The marinade adds a burst of bold flavours and cooks in minutes with the intense heat keeping all the juices intact. Made with a fusion of Indian spices, lemon juice and prawns which are griddled to perfection. A delicious zingy starter, a satisfying snack or even more delectable on the BBQ.

**SERVES 2**

## INGREDIENTS

- *250g raw jumbo king prawns, deveined and shelled*
- *1 tbsp sunflower oil*
- *1 tsp garlic paste*
- *½ tsp green chilli paste*
- *1 tsp tomato puree*
- *½ tsp red wine vinegar*
- *1 tsp tandoori powder*
- *1 tsp Kashmiri chilli powder*
- *Juice of ¼ of a lemon*
- *1 tsp turmeric*
- *½ tsp salt, or to taste*
- *¼ tsp cracked black pepper*
- *½ tsp coriander powder*
- *½ tsp ground cumin*
- *Chopped fresh coriander for garnish*

## METHOD

Place the prawns in a mixing bowl and add all the ingredients. Marinate for 2 hours.

I like to use a griddled pan to get that charred effect. Heat oil in the pan. Make sure the pan is smoking hot so that the prawns will sizzle when they touch the pan.

You can put the prawns on wooden skewers, or simply cook them as they are. Place the prawns gently on the hot pan. Cook for 3-4 minutes turning halfway. Once cooked, garnish with coriander.

Serve with a coriander and mint chutney and a side salad.

PILCHARDS CURRY

# PILCHARDS CURRY

A curry made from tinned fish that is so full of flavour and has an almost umami vibe that easily makes it one of my top quick go to meals. This recipe is great for those days when you're short on time or the fridge is looking a little scarce. All that's needed are tomatoes, an onion and some spices, and dinners ready! This is one I learned and adapted from my mother-in-law as my husband grew up on it.

**SERVES 2**

## INGREDIENTS

- *3 tbsp sunflower oil*
- *¼ tsp fenugreek seeds*
- *½ tsp garlic paste*
- *1 x 400g tin Pilchards in tomato sauce*
- *¼ tsp turmeric*
- *½ tsp red chilli powder*
- *½ tsp salt*
- *¼ tsp garam masala*
- *100ml water*
- *1 tomato (finely chopped)*
- *Freshly chopped coriander for garnish*

## METHOD

Heat oil on a medium heat a wide frying pan, add fenugreek seeds and fry for a minute or so until they become slightly darker in colour. Be careful not to burn the seeds as this will give a bitter taste to your curry. Add garlic and swirl around in the oil with the fenugreek seeds.

In a large bowl empty the contents of the tinned pilchards. Carefully remove the fish from the tomato sauce into a separate plate. Now add the tomato sauce to the frying pan. Stir well with the garlic. To this add turmeric, red chilli powder, salt and garam masala and mix well. Add 100ml water to the pan, bring to a simmer and continue to cook on a medium heat for 10-12 minutes until the sauce thickens, but doesn't dry out. Add a splash of water if looks too dry. Whilst the sauce is simmering away, slowly remove the bones from the pilchards.

Gently add the pilchards to the simmering sauce skin down. Careful not to break the fish as its very tender. Gently spoon

Add finely chopped tomatoes and simmer for a few more minutes. Garnish with freshly chopped coriander and serve with rice.

# INDIAN BREADS

# CHAPATI'S

Chapati, also known as roti or rotli, are an everyday staple within an Indian household. Traditionally a chapati is rolled out using a patlo (wooden board) and a velan (thin rolling pin), then cooked on a cast iron tava. Coming home to smell of fresh, warm, buttery chapati's is a childhood memory that will live with me forever. They bring me so much comfort and joy, and I hope they do to you too!

**MAKES 6 CHAPATI'S**

## INGREDIENTS

- *200g Chapati flour (I suggest medium wholewheat chapatti flour) + extra for dusting*
- *2 tbsp Sunflower oil + 1 tsp*
- *120ml boiling hot water*
- *Butter or ghee for the cooked chapati's*

## METHOD

Prepare the dough by adding sunflower oil to the chapati flour in a mixing bowl. Rub the oil into the flour using your finger tips. Make a well in the middle and add 120ml of boiling water, either boiled in a pan or in the kettle. Use a spoon at this point to initially combine the water into the flour mixture as it will be too hot to touch. After a minute or so you should be able to use your hands to start kneading the dough for 2-3 minutes until you have a soft and smooth dough ball. Drizzle another 1 tsp of oil the dough and smooth over the dough gently with your hands. Cover the bowl of dough with a towel and leave for 5 minutes.

Now knead the dough one last time for 10-15 seconds. Divide the dough into 6 equal little dough balls. Take a piece of dough and roll it between your palms and flatten it slightly. Dip each side into chapati flour. Now begin rolling your dough in a circular motion. Years of practice have taught me to roll a round chapati using the rolling pin to move the dough in circular motions. Believe me I don't expect anyone to be able to do this without practice. The easiest way to do this is to pick the chapati up with one hand and move it around yourself. Create an even surface, perfectly round chapati approx. 8 inches in diameter.

Preheat your tawa over medium to low heat for 5 minutes. Place the rolled out chapati onto the tawa and cook for approx 10-15 seconds until little bubbles appear on the surface then flip it. Cook for a further 30 seconds. If you lift the chapati you will see the underside has little brown spots all over. At this point flip it again and cook for 10 – 15 seconds more until more darker spots appear. This is the stage where the chapati should rise. Don't worry if they don't rise initially. It will come with practice. Flip the chapati one last time and place on this side up on kitchen tissue. Spread with plenty of butter or ghee.

Repeat this process for the remaining dough balls until you have a perfect stack. Serve immediately whist warm to scoop up some delicious dal or the gravy of your favourite curry.

*Example of Chapati Making*

MASALA PARATHA

# MASALA PARATHA

An easy flatbread recipe with some added spice to give a real flavour punch. They are deliciously crispy and flaky, and can be enjoyed in a matter of minutes for breakfast or lunch.

**SERVES 2-3**

## INGREDIENTS

- *300g chapati flour, plus extra for dusting*
- *2 tbsp sunflower oil, plus extra during rolling and cooking*
- *¼ tsp turmeric*
- *Masala mix made up of 3 tsp red chilli powder and 1 tsp salt*
- *150ml hot water*

## METHOD

In a large mixing bowl combine the chapati flour with 2 tbsp of sunflower oil. Rub the oil into the flour using your fingertips. Stir through the turmeric. Now add the hot water and knead the dough well. The dough should be smooth and soft. Lightly grease the dough with a touch of oil, cover the bowl with a tea towel and rest for 15 minutes.

Gently knead the dough again and divide the dough into 6 equal balls.

Place a tava/frying pan on medium-low heat. It will reach the desired temperature while you're rolling the parathas.

Dust one of the balls with chapati flour and roll into a small circle, approx. 6" in diameter. Lightly brush the surface with sunflower oil and sprinkle ½ tsp of the masala mix over the chapati surface. Now fold the chapati in half, then in half again to create a quarter moon shape. Roll out the masala filled dough to approx. 7-8" in diameter. Visually it will look like a rounded triangle. Repeat for each dough ball.

Place the rolled paratha onto the hot tava/ frying pan. Cook for a minute before flipping to cook the other side for a minute. Drizzle the surface of the paratha with sunflower oil and flip again. Press slightly with a flat spatula, drizzle again with sunflower oil and flip. Gently pressing with the flat spatula, continue to flip until both sides are cooked with patches browned and crisp.

Repeat for each rolled paratha.

Serve the masala paratha with chai for breakfast, or with plain yogurt and pickles for a snack.

TIKHI POORI

# TIKHI PURI

This is a spicy version of the regular puri which calls for the addition of Indian spices like turmeric powder which lends the puri its's lovely yellow shade. As a child this was a vegetarian breakfast special in our house. These and a good old cup of Indian chai. It's a comforting breakfast/midday snack.

**WILL MAKE APPROX. 40 PURI'S**

## INGREDIENTS

- *300g chapati flour*
- *½ tsp turmeric*
- *1 tsp green chilli paste*
- *½ tsp garlic paste*
- *¾ tsp salt, or to taste*
- *2 tbsp oil*
- *160ml boiling water*
- *Oil for deep frying*

## METHOD

In a large mixing bowl add the chapati flour, turmeric, green chilli paste, garlic paste and salt. Mix well. Now add the oil and using your fingertip rub into the flour mix. Now add the water and combine well and knead to form a smooth soft dough. Cover the dough with a tea towel and rest for 10 minutes. If you have a stiff hard dough then your puri's will not puff up, and if your dough is too soft then they will absorb too much oil during frying making then oily.

Divide the dough into small cherry tomato size balls

Heat oil on a medium heat in a wok for deep frying, approx. 190 degrees.

Roll each dough ball into small 2-3 inch diameter round puri's. Don't roll them too thin.

Once the oil is hot (you will know this if you [place a pinch of the puri dough into the oil it should sizzle and rice to the surface of the oil), carefully place 2 puri's into the oil and start to fry them. Using a slotted frying spoon, gently tap the puri on top so that they puff up. Flip on to the other side and fry until they turn a light golden colour. Transfer the puri to paper towel lined dish to drain any excess oil. Repeat for the remaining puri's. Fry 2 at a time as overcrowding the oil will cause the temperature of the oil to reduce.

The puri's should be beautifully golden and dry. Best served fresh with a mango drink and for a delicious snack. They will store well in an airtight container for 2 days, great with masala chai the next day.

# BHAKRI

Bhakri is a delicious thick flatbread made from chapati flour. They have a crispy, flaky outer layer and soft inside. You can enjoy these with pickles, or with your dinner. Goes beautiful with my Gujrati Kanda Bateta. When I was little I used to sneakily eat all the crispy flaky outer layer of the bhakri and leave the remaining soft inner layer in the chapati tin for my dad to eat. He'd say which undarr (mouse) has been to nibbling at these. Sometimes I would do it just for this reaction.

**MAKES 6 BAKRI**

## INGREDIENTS

- *200g Chapati flour*
- *4 tbsp sunflower oil + oil for cooking*
- *100ml hot boiling water*

## METHOD

To make the bhakri, add oil to the chapati flour and rub together using your finger tips. Now gradually add boiling water and knead into a stiff dough. If the dough was soft like chapati dough then the bhakri's will not be crispy on the outside.

Divide the dough into 6 equal portions. Using a rolling pin roll into round thick cirlces, approx 5 inches in diameter.

Heat a tava or cast iron pan on medium-low heat. Place one of the rolled out bhakri's onto the hot tava. As light brown spots appear flip the bhakri to lightly brown the other side too. Now flip again and gently pour a tsp or oil around the edges of the bhakri. Using a large spatula put gentle pressure onto the bhakri. It may even puff up slightly. After 10-15 seconds flip and crisp up the other side too. Repeat this process for all the bhakri's.

# THEPLA (FENUGREEK FLATBREADS)

Fenugreek has such a bold flavour and pair it with these simple ingredients will create the perfect lunch snack. These light feathery flatbreads are the perfect start to any weekend and the most satisfying' on the go' snack as it's also full of iron. One of my favourite treats is to roll one up and dip it in my Indian chai. Give it a go - it will most definitely wake you up!

# THEPLA (FENUGREEK FLATBREADS)

**MAKES 8 FLATBREADS**
**SERVES 2-4**

## INGREDIENTS

- *400g medium chapati flour (I normally use a medium grade chapati flour) + extra during rolling*
- *1 tbsp chickpea flour*
- *1 ½ tbsp sunflower oil + more for cooking*
- *1 tsp turmeric*
- *1 tsp salt, or to taste*
- *1 tsp garlic paste*
- *1 tsp green chilli paste*
- *100g fresh fenugreek leaves – finely chopped*
- *2 tbsp set/hung yogurt*
- *2 tbsp hot water*

## METHOD

In a mixing bowl combine all the ingredient, apart from the water. Use your fingertips to blend all the spices and methi leaves into the flours. Now add the yogurt and water. Mix and knead into a dough. Don't add water while kneading as the methi leaves will release water. Knead into a soft dough that is not sticky. Once you have a nice soft dough, smear a few drops of oil over the dough, cover with a damp tea towel and rest for 20 minutes.

Now divide the dough into 8 equal sized balls. Take a piece of dough and flatten slightly with the palm of your hands. Before rolling out the flatbreads, heat a tawa or frying pan over a low heat. This will reach the correct temperature by the time you have rolled out your thepla's.

Take one of the dough pieces and dip into chapati flour ensuring all sides are covered. Roll with your rolling pin into a large circle, approx. 8" in diameter. Not too thin, otherwise they will turn crisp when baking. Roll them all out at set to one side.

Your tawa/frying pan should be hot enough now. Turn the heat up to medium. Transfer one of your rolled thepla on to the tawa. Cook until you see small bubbles, flip and cook on the other side. Press gently with a spatula. Drizzle half a tsp of sunflower oil on either side of the flatbreads and cook until they start to turn golden in colour with brown spots on the surface on the thepla. Transfer to a tissue paper lined dish or tin. Repeat this process for the remaining thepla. Enjoy with a pickle of your choice and plain yogurt. Or perfect with your morning cup of masala chai.

If you store these thepla in a lined tin/container they will keep for a couple of days. Alternatively, you can place in the fridge and reheat in the microwave for 10-15 seconds as and when.

They also freeze really well for a rainy day. Place a piece of parchment paper between each thepla and stack. Wrap them all together in aluminium foil. Simply defrost before reheating in the microwave.

# BHATURA

These puri like breads are addictive! They go perfectly with Chana Chole. There are many variations of making these crispy and fluffy deep-fried breads. My recipe is simple and does not need yeast therefore eliminates the need for fermentation. The addition of chilli flakes impart an irresistible smoky note, and the addition of fresh coriander gives a beautiful flavour and colour to the bhatura. I can quite happily eat my way through these on their own. You need to eat them while they are warm and fresh.

## BHATURA

**MAKES 6 MEDIUM SIZED BHATURA'S**
**SERVES 3-4**

### INGREDIENTS

- *250g plain flour*
- *3 tbsp breadcrumbs (You can make your own with 1 slice of dried stale bread)*
- *1 tsp red chilli flakes*
- *30g bunch of freshly chopped coriander. Needs to be dry, not wet. Pat dry with a towel.*
- *¾ tbsp ghee*
- *1 tsp salt, or to taste*
- *130ml Warm water – I normally use boiled kettle water.*
- *Sunflower oil for deep frying*

### METHOD

In a mixing bowl add the flour and ghee. Rub together between your fingers making sure there are no clumps. Add the breadcrumbs, red chilli flakes, salt and fresh coriander. Mix all the ingredient together. Now slowly add the water and knead for a good 5 minutes into a soft and smooth dough. Add more water if you feel if needs it. The dough should not sticky or too firm.

On a medium heat, place a wok or kadai ¾ of way filled with sunflower oil. You will know when the oil is ready, if you drop a small piece of dough into the oil and it comes up to the top briskly (about 180 degrees). That's when the oil is ready to fry the bhatura.

Divide the dough into 6 equal balls. Roll in the palms of your hands, getting rid of any creases. Using a rolling pin, roll each ball into a circular shape, not too thin, slightly thicker than a tortilla wrap. Add the rolled bhatura to the hot oil and using a slotted spoon keep spinning the bhatura in a circular motion until it starts to puff up, flip gently to fry the other side until both sides are brown.

Place the fried bhatura on tissue paper to drain any excess oil. Serve with my delicious Chana Chole *(page 80)*.

# GARLIC AND CORIANDER NAAN

This is a soft, fluffy and delicious naan recipe that requires no yeast! Feel free to eat them plain without the garlic and coriander. The perfect accompaniment to mop up any curry with a recipe which could not be easier.

## GARLIC AND CORIANDER NAAN

**8 MEDIUM SIZED NAANS**
**SERVES 3-4**

### INGREDIENTS

- *200g self-raising flour (some extra for dusting)*
- *50g plain yogurt (or you can use a dairy-free alternative)*
- *50ml water*
- *¾ tsp salt, or to taste*
- *Pinch of baking soda*
- *2 tbsp of sunflower oil*
- *1 tsp garlic paste*
- *1 tsp black nigella seeds*
- *2 tbsp finely chopped coriander*
- *Softened butter for brushing cooked naans*

### METHOD

Add the flour to a mixing bowl and mix in the salt and baking soda. Add the garlic paste, finely chopped coriander, nigella seeds and oil. Rub the ingredients using your fingertips into the flour and salt mix.

In a separate bowl mix together yogurt and water to create a runny mixture. Pour over the flour mix and Knead the dough for a good 5 minutes into a soft, smooth dough ball. Cover and rest for 5-10 minutes.

You should be able to make roughly 8 small naans from this. Divide the dough into 8 equal dough balls. On a lightly floured surface, with a rolling pin roll one of the dough balls into a fairly thin, roundish oblong shape. Don't worry if it's not perfect. Heat a non-stick frying pan over medium-low heat, lay one of the rolled-out naans into the pan. You don't need any additional oil to cook them. Cook for 2 minutes each side until lightly charred. Brush the naans with butter and enjoy this yummy goodness.

# ALOO PARATHA

The aroma of an Aloo Paratha can never leave you. A crispy layer of dough stuffed with a blend of spices combined with potato will give you all the comfort you ever need with this classic.

# ALOO PARATHA

**SERVES 2-3**

## INGREDIENTS FOR 6 PARATHAS

### For the paratha filling

- *3 medium potatoes, skin peeled, boiled and mashed*
- *1 small red onion*
- *½ tsp green chilli paste*
- *½ tsp garlic paste*
- *½ tsp ginger paste*
- *½ tsp turmeric*
- *¼ tsp ground cumin*
- *2 tbsp finely chopped fresh coriander*
- *½ tsp salt*

### For the paratha dough

- *400g of chapati*
- *150-300ml warm water to knead the dough (boiled kettle water)*
- *3 tbsp oil*
- *½ tsp salt*
- *1 tsp nigella seeds*

## METHOD

First make the dough so you can let it rest before rolling.

In a mixing bowl, mix the flour, salt and nigella seeds. Add the oil and rub into the flour mixture. Add the warm water little at a time mixing with a spoon. Now knead with hands to make a soft and smooth dough. If you add too much water, it will become sticky. If that happens, don't worry, add a little bit more chapati flour to perfect the dough. Drizzle the dough with a small amount of oil and massage through the dough to prevent it from drying out. Cover with a wet tea towel and rest for 15 minutes. For the filling, add all the ingredients to the mashed potato. Mix till everything is well combined. The paratha filling is now ready. Put the frying pan or tawa on a very low heat to warm ready for cooking the parathas. Divide the dough into 6 equal dough balls.

Dust the surface with some chapati flour, take one of the dough balls and roll into a small circle using your rolling pin. Brush with a little oil. Take 3 tbsp's of the paratha filling and place in the centre of the rolled circle dough. Take care not to overfill otherwise it will become difficult to roll again. Bring all the edges together of the rolled-out dough, fully enclosing the filling inside. Now gently flatten the dough using the palm of your hands. Dust the surface again with some more chapati flour and, roll the filled dough into a 7-inch approx. diameter circle. Having a gentle hand is key as it will help create an even surface and you roll around all the edges. Repeat the same process for the remaining dough. Place each rolled paratha on a dry tea towel ready for cooking.

Now turn the flame of the frying pan/tawa onto medium heat. Transfer one of the rolled parathas onto the pan. Cook for a couple of minutes and then flip over and cook for another minute. Drizzle ½ tsp of oil to the top of the paratha and flip. Apply the same amount of oil to the other side. Apply gentle pressure with a wooden spatula. Be careful not to apply too much pressure otherwise you will force the filling out of the dough. Flip the paratha again. Cook until both sides of the paratha look golden in colour.

Serve the parathas warm with my carrot pickle *(page 182)*. I normally like to make these at weekends for lunch.

If you are lucky enough to have leftovers, my parathas taste delicious the day after. I like to sprinkle the top of a paratha with some finely grated mature cheddar (sprinkle with red chilli flakes if you fancy an extra kick). Pop under the grill until the cheese starts to melt and the edges of the paratha start to crisp up. All that's left to do is indulge!

# RICE

# PILAU RICE

Be prepared for a serious adventure of taste when it comes to this dish. The fragrance of this rice will send you into a spin and the taste will blow your mind. You can prepare the spices in small bags ready to infuse your rice at the drop of a hat. Instantly creating something spectacular to enjoy with a dish of dal. It will also leave your home smelling delightfully warm with that clove and cardamom scent.

**SERVES 2**

## INGREDIENTS

- *200g long grain basmati rice*
- *525ml hot water*
- *½ tsp Salt, or to taste*
- *1 tsp cumin seeds*
- *1 tbsp sunflower oil*
- *2 tbsp cashew nuts, split in half*
- *3-4 cardamom pods*
- *1 medium sized cinnamon stick*
- *4-5 black peppercorns*
- *3-4 cloves*
- *3 bay leaves*
- *A handful of garden peas*

## METHOD

Firstly, heat the oil in a saucepan on a very low heat, add cumin seeds, cardamom pods, cinnamon stick, peppercorns, cloves and bay leaf. Continuously stir for a minute then add the cashew nuts. Now add the rice and garden peas and mix gently with the oil and whole spices. Be gentle as to not break the rice. Now add the hot water and stir in the salt. Turn the heat up to a medium to high flame to get the water bubbling. Now turn the heat back down to low, cover the pan with a lid and simmer until all the water has evaporated and the rice is perfectly cooked.

# CHICKEN PULAO

A one pot chicken and rice dish made with cloves, cardamom, garlic, ginger and caramelised onions. Requires very little effort and makes a soul satisfying dinner. Mildly spiced with aromatics and not heavy like a traditional biriyani.

**SERVES 4**

## INGREDIENTS

- *1kg chicken on the bone, skinless and cut into medium sized chunks*
- *3 onions, sliced*
- *250g long grain basmati rice*
- *500ml warm water*
- *4 tbsp sunflower oil*
- *5-6 cloves*
- *4 green cardamom pods*
- *1 cinnamon stick*
- *1 ½ tsp cumin seeds*
- *¾ tsp crushed black peppercorns*
- *1 ½ tsp coriander powder*
- *1 ½ tsp salt, or to taste*
- *4 green chillies, slit down the middle lengthways*
- *2 tsp garlic paste*
- *2 tsp ginger paste*
- *Chopped fresh coriander for garnish*
- *Lime for garnish*

## METHOD

In a heavy bottom wide saucepan, heat the sunflower oil on medium heat and add the cloves, cardamom pods and cinnamon stick. Swirl them around in the oil. Let them sizzle then add the cumin seeds. Cook for a few more seconds until they release an aroma. Now reduce the heat to low and add the sliced onions. Cook, stirring often until they are soft and lightly caramelised. Now add the slit green chillies and mix with the onions for a few seconds. Now add the coriander powder, ginger and garlic pastes, stir and sauté for 5 minutes for they infuse with the onions. Now add the chicken pieces, stir and combine well with all the spices and onions. Cook for 10-12 minutes. Add 200ml of the water, turn the heat up ever so slightly and simmer with the lid on for a further 10-12 minutes. Now add the basmati rice and the rest of the water. Simmer for 20 minutes with the lid on until all the water has evaporated, and the rice is cooked through and the chicken is cooked through and tender. Turn off the heat and allow the chicken pulao to rest.

When you're ready to serve, fluff up the rice with a fork and serve with a generous garnishing of coriander and a squeeze of fresh lime. Serve with a simple carrot and cucumber raita.

# PLAIN WHITE RICE

This is the easiest way to cook rice in a pan (No fussing around). I find myself cooking rice a couple of times a week and I've been making rice this way for as long as I can remember. It's the best fool proof way!

**SERVES 2**

## INGREDIENTS

- *200g white basmati rice (washed)*
- *400ml hot water*
- *Salt*
- *Sunflower oil*

## METHOD

Add all the ingredients to a saucepan. Bring the open pan to a rapid boil over high heat. Boil unit you have approx. 1 inch of water above rice level left. Reduce the heat to low, place the lid on the pan and cook for approx. 8-12 minutes until all the water has evaporated. Turn the heat off and let the rice rest for 10 minutes with the lid on to allow the rice to steam. Don't sneak a peek, be patient.

Now using a fork gently fluff up the rice to separate the grains and serve.

You can quite easily turn this into Jeera Rice by adding 1 tbsp of jeera seeds to the ingredients.

You can also make mixed vegetable rice by adding 4 tbsp of chopped frozen vegetables (carrots, peas, sweetcorn) to the ingredients listed.

# LAMB DUM BIRIYANI

Tender morsels of lamb are marinated then cooked with rice. To 'dum' the biriyani means to seal the pot with a dough and steam cook, so when you break into it, it releases unforgettable aromas. Everyone has a unique way of making biriyani. There is no right or wrong way but the most important part is the flavouring of the meat and rice. An authentic meal with an amazing blend of spices your whole family will love. This is a labour of love, but you will not be disappointed!

**SERVES 4-6**

## INGREDIENTS

### Lamb marinade

- *1kg of lamb shoulder*
- *4 tbsp set yogurt*
- *1 heaped tbsp tomato puree*
- *3 tbsp oil*
- *1 tsp turmeric*
- *2 tsp red chilli powder*
- *1 tsp cumin powder*
- *1 tsp coriander powder*
- *¾ tsp salt, or to taste*
- *¾ tsp black pepper powder*
- *1 tsp garam masala*

### Masala base

- *4 tbsp sunflower oil*
- *2 medium onions, finely sliced*
- *3 medium tomatoes, finely chopped*
- *4 green chillies, finely sliced*
- *¼ tsp salt*

### Rice

- *500g long grain basmati rice, washed and drained*
- *1 tbsp sunflower oil*
- *Water to cook the rice*
- *3 bay leaves*
- *2 medium sticks of cinnamon*
- *6-7 cloves*
- *3 green cardamom pods*
- *1 tbsp caraway seeds*
- *1 tbsp cumin seeds*
- *1 ½ tsp salt, or to taste*

### For the chapati dough lid

- *400g chapati flour*
- *2 tbsp sunflower oil*
- *210ml warm water*

### Other ingredients

- *2 medium onions, thinly sliced for frying*
- *Sunflower oil for frying*
- *6 baby potatoes, peeled*
- *2 tbsp raisins*
- *3 tbsp fresh coriander, finely chopped*
- *2 tbsp fresh mint leave, finely chopped*
- *1 tbsp Fresh green garlic (optional)*
- *4-5 saffron strands, soaked in 3 tbsp of warm milk*

## METHOD

Firstly, marinate the lamb in the ingredient listed for the lamb marinade. Marinate for 2+ hours, or overnight in the fridge if possible. Remove from the fridge 30 minutes before cooking.

In a large saucepan heat oil on a medium heat from the listed ingredients for the 'rice'. To the oil add the bay leaves, cardamom pods, cinnamon sticks and cloves. Swirl around the oil to release the aroma. Now turn the heat down to low, add the cumin seeds, caraway seeds and sizzle for a few seconds before adding the washed rice. gently mix without breaking the rice. Now add salt and enough warm water to fill the pan ¾ of the way. Give it one last stir, turn the heat up to high and bring to boil and cook the rice until the grains feel like they 70% cooked. Drain the rice and then you need to cool the rice down by spreading out large spoonful's of the partly cooked rice into a few large serving dishes. This will stop the rice going mushy when layering as a biriyani.

From the 'other ingredients' list, heat sunflower oil in a frying pan for shallow frying the 2 medium onions, finely sliced. Fry handfuls at a time until golden brown. Drain on kitchen paper and set to a side for later.

Use 4 tbsp of this frying oil to assemble the ingredients in the 'masala base' list. Place the oil in a pan on medium heat and add the 2 finely sliced onions, sauté and slightly brown. Now add the ginger paste and garlic paste and sauté for 5 minutes with the onions. Now add the chopped tomatoes, finely sliced green chillies, salt and cook for 8-10 minutes until the tomatoes become soft and mushy.

Now you can the marinated lamb shoulder to the pan of masala base. Mix well on a low heat until all the ingredients are combined. Now add the peeled baby potatoes, raisins and mix well again. Turn the heat up to medium, place a lid on the pan and cook for approx. 30-35 minutes, stirring occasionally until the potatoes are cooked and the lamb is tenderised. Take off the heat once cooked.

Now everything is prepared you can start to layer for the biriyani. Grease a large oven proof dish with some oil. Add the first layer of cooked rice (inclusive of dry spices). On top of the rice gently add a layer of the lamb curry masala base. Add a flourish of the fried onions. Garnish with chopped fresh coriander, mint and green garlic. Repeat the process twice again. The top layer should finish with the rice. Drizzle over the saffron infused milk.

Prepare the chapati dough lid but combining the chapati flour and oil. Then pour over the warm water to knead to a dough. Roll out the dough large enough to cover the top of your dish. Keep a thickness of 2-3mm of the rolled dough.

Cover the dish with your rolled out chapati dough, securely sealing the edges. Place in a preheated oven of 180 degrees for 25-30 minutes until the chapati dough lid has turned golden.

Carefully remove/break the dough lid releasing the steam. Enjoy immediately with raita and kachumber salad.

# TOOR DAL KHICHDI

A healthy, simple and humble Indian dish made with rice and dal so wholesome and light. Serve with a pickle on the side. My mum would make this if we were feeling under the weather. This is also one of the first foods I weaned my babies on (minus the salt).

**SERVES 4**

## INGREDIENTS

- *200g rice*
- *75g toor dal*
- *600ml hot water*
- *½ tsp turmeric*
- *1 tsp salt, or to taste*
- *1 tbsp sunflower oil*

## METHOD

Wash and soak the toor dal in warm water for 2 hours. Drain and add to a medium sized saucepan. Wash and drain the rice and add the toor dal in the saucepan. Now add salt, turmeric and sunflower oil. Gently mix together, careful not to break the rice. Now add 600ml of hot kettle water. Place the saucepan on the stove and boil on a high heat until you have approx. half a centimetre of water left above the rice level. Turn the heat right down to low, put a lid on the pan and cook for 10-15 minutes until the water has been completely absorbed and the khichdi is soft and cooked. Turn the heat off and let the rice rest with the lid on for 15 minutes. Fluff the rice up with a spoon before serving with a big dollop of ghee. Pour some khadi over the khichdi and serve with any of my dishes, particularly my veggie dishes.

# SALADS AND PICKLES

CARROT SALAD

# CARROT SALAD

Take a carrot salad to the next level with simple store cupboard ingredients. You can make this refreshing salad in minutes. A classic recipe that everyone can enjoy. I enjoy healthy food, but that doesn't mean it has to be a variety of dull greens all day.

**SERVES 2**

## INGREDIENTS

- *200g grated/matchstick carrots*
- *½ finely diced red onion*
- *50g raisins*
- *50g roasted cashews*
- *Chopped parsley for garnish*

## INGREDIENTS FOR THE DRESSING

- *3 tbsp olive oil*
- *2 tbsp honey*
- *¼ tsp garlic paste*
- *1 tsp ginger paste*
- *2 tbsp fresh lime juice*
- *1 tsp turmeric*
- *Zest of half an orange*
- *Zest of half a lime*
- *Coarsely ground black pepper*
- *Pinch of salt, or to taste*

## METHOD

Mix all the ingredients for the dressing. It's quite a thick dressing, so don't worry if it isn't runny like you'd expect a dressing to be.

In a large mixing bowl add the carrots and onions. Pour the dressing in. give it a good mix. I normally like to get my hands in but use a wooden spoon. Then toss in the raisins, cashews, and parsley. Leave a little bit of parsley to sprinkle over the top when serving. Can be eaten as a light lunch, with some grilled chicken, or as an accompaniment at barbeques. It's a crowd pleaser either way.

MUNG BEAN SALAD

# MUNG BEAN SALAD

If you haven't heard or tried the incredible mung bean yet, then now's the time to impress your guests with this simple yet divine side salad. A refreshingly mouth-watering explosion of flavour, which offers a textured crunch and a subtle nutty flavour. As well as being tasty, the mung beans are packed with protein, fibre, and antioxidants.

**SERVES 2**

## INGREDIENTS

- *400g sprouted mung beans ("Sprout Your Own Lentils" on pg 12)*
- *1 red onion*
- *1 boiled and cubed sweet potato*
- *Half finely diced red pepper*
- *8 – 10 Coloured baby plum tomatoes halved*
- *1 finely chopped red chilli*
- *½ tsp cayenne pepper*
- *1 and ½ tsp lemon juice*
- *Chopped fresh coriander for garnish*
- *Cracked black pepper*
- *Pinch of salt*

## METHOD

Simply put all the above ingredients into a mixing bowl and mix until fully combined. Sprinkle with coriander and serve.

# AVOCADO AND FETA SMASH SALAD

A simple to assemble, great healthy snack, packed with crunchy textures with freshness and surprising flavours.

**SERVES 2-3**

## INGREDIENTS

- *2 ripe avocados*
- *2 tsp lemon juice*
- *Half red pepper*
- *Half yellow pepper*
- *1 small red onion, finely chopped*
- *1 finely chopped red chilli*
- *½ tsp red chilli flakes*
- *¼ tsp coarsely ground black pepper*
- *Coarsely ground sea salt, to taste*
- *50g feta cheese*
- *Finely chopped coriander*

## METHOD

Firstly, flame grill/roast the red and yellow pepper until charred. Finely chop the charred pepper and set a side.

Now dice the avocado, add to a mixing bowl. Using the back of a fork, roughly mash the avocado, leaving some chunks.

To the mixing bowl add the charred chopped pepper, chopped red onion and mix. Now add the finely chopped chilli, red chilli flakes, sea salt and black pepper, and lemon juice. Mix all the ingredients together gently. Now crumble in the feta and sprinkle over some finely chopped coriander.

You can simply eat this with a garden salad. I like to eat this topped on lightly toasted sourdough, or even make a quesadilla out of it.

# SUMMERY MANGO CHAAT

The perfect combo if you love mango with the added kick of chaat masala. Fresh ingredients tossed together with simple seasoning will surely tickle your tastebuds and leave you craving more. It's an easy, effortless recipe that is flavourful and a crunchy delight!

**SERVES 2**

## INGREDIENTS

- *1 mango, cut into cm cubes*
- *1 ripe avocado, cut into cm cubes*
- *1 red onion, finely chopped*
- *100g cherry tomatoes, slice each one into 3 pieces*
- *1 red chilli, finely sliced*
- *2 tbsp finely chopped coriander*
- *Juice of 1 lime*
- *Pinch of sea salt*
- *Pinch of chaat masala*
- *fine Sev – fried gram noodles (readily available in supermarkets and Indian food stores)*

## METHOD

Assemble all the listed ingredients in a bowl serve as a side dish.

Optional - Sprinkle with chaat masala and fine Sev. It's light and refreshing. Perfect for bbq's.

# KACHUMBER SALAD

Variations of this can be found all over the world in different cuisines. A combination of onions, tomatoes and cucumber.

Add some freshness to your meal with this easy and delicious Indian staple. A simple salad that will accompany any Indian dish!

**SERVES 2**

## INGREDIENTS

- *1 red onion, finely sliced,*
- *2 tomatoes, finely chopped*
- *Half of a large cucumber, finely diced*
- *Pomegranate seeds from half a pomegranate*
- *1 tsp lemon juice*
- *Salt and pepper, season according to taste*
- *1 tbsp fresh coriander, finely chopped*

## METHOD

In a large mixing bowl combine the onions, tomatoes and cucumber. Add the lemon juice and season with salt and pepper. Now toss through the pomegranate seeds and garnish with finely chopped coriander.

Serve as a side salad to any meal.

# SPICY INDIAN SLAW

A colourful, fresh slaw with a kick. Makes a great side dish for so many different recipes. Refreshing and tasty.

**SERVES 4**

## INGREDIENTS

- *5tbsp low fat Greek yogurt*
- *200g carrots, coarsely grated*
- *¼ red cabbage, shredded*
- *1 red onion, finely sliced*
- *2 red chillies, finely sliced*
- *1 lime, juice and zest*
- *½ tsp cumin seeds, roasted*
- *2 tbsp fresh coriander, finely chopped*
- *2 tbsp unsalted peanuts, toasted*
- *Salt and pepper to taste*

## METHOD

In a large bowl, mix the carrots, cabbage, red onion and chillies.

In a small bowl/jug make the dressing by adding the yogurt, lime juice, cumin seeds and season with salt and pepper, and stir together well. Pour the dressing over the veggies in the large bowl. Combine everything together well.

Stir in the freshly chopped coriander, and toasted peanuts. Grate over some lime zest and serve.

# CARROT PICKLE

Put it on your papadums as a starter, or it can also be eaten with any of my veggie dishes!

**SERVES 4**

## INGREDIENTS

- *3 medium carrots*
- *2 tbsp methia masala/aachar masala (basically an Indian pickle masala)*
- *2 tbsp olive oil*
- *¼ tsp salt*

## METHOD

Peel the carrots and cut into 2 inch long thin pieces. Place them in a bowl and sprinkle with the salt. Leave for approx. 3 hours. You will notice the salt has drawn the moisture from the carrots.

Once you've let the carrots rest in the salt for 3 hours or so, transfer to a paper towel and pat down any excess water. Put the carrots in a tray evenly spaced out and place the tray in a warm and dry area of your house for a good 12-24 hours, until they start to look slightly dehydrated. You don't want them too dry otherwise you'll have yourself a very chewy pickle. No one wants a chewy pickle.

Now transfer the slightly dehydrated carrots to a mixing bowl and add the olive oil, ensuring all the carrots are coated well in the oil. Now add the methia masala and toss the carrots well in all the masala to fully coat them. Transfer to an airtight jar and refrigerate. It will last for up to 4 weeks.

Try it with my parathas – it's mind-blowingly amazing.

# CUCUMBER KACHUMBER

This is such a popular simple side salad served in many Indian households to accompany any authentic Indian meal. This kachumber is very basic and easy to make. I love to whip up fast and simple salads, but it's got to be tasty and pack a punch. Not essential, but even better if made ahead of time to let the flavours of the chilli infuse into cucumber.

**SERVES 4**

## INGREDIENTS

- *½ cucumber*
- *1 tsp lemon juice*
- *½ tsp green chilli paste*
- *Finely chopped coriander for garnish*

## METHOD

Cut and slice the cucumber length ways into 1 inch pieces. Add the lemon juice. Add the green chilli paste and coat the cucumber well in the chilli paste. Toss in some finely chopped coriander and refrigerate until ready to serve.

# RAITA'S, DIPS AND CHUTNEY'S

CORIANDER AND MINT CHUTNEY

# CORIANDER AND MINT CHUTNEY

Coriander and mint are a match made in heaven which can go well with any starter or side dish.

**SERVES 4**

## INGREDIENTS

- *100g coriander, chopped*
- *50g mint leaves*
- *1 garlic clove*
- *2 green chilli*
- *Juice of ½ lime*
- *½ tsp cumin powder*
- *½ tsp coriander powder*
- *4 tbsp water*
- *Salt, as per taste*

## METHOD

Add all the listed ingredients to a blender and blend into a vibrant green paste. Season with salt and stir.

# GREEN PEANUT CHUTNEY

A tasty chutney which will go with many different types of food, however, makes a great accompaniment to kebabs.

**SERVES 4**

## INGREDIENTS

- *200g coriander, chopped*
- *1 green pepper, chopped*
- *4 garlic cloves*
- *2 green chillies*
- *2 tbsp unsalted skinless peanuts, coarsely ground*
- *1 tsp granulated sugar*
- *2 tsp lime juice*
- *¼ tsp salt, or to taste*
- *25ml groundnut oil*

## METHOD

In a blender, add coriander, green pepper, garlic cloves, green chillies and salt. Blend to a pulp. Add lime juice, granulated sugar and coarsely ground peanuts. Stir together with the groundnut oil.

# CORIANDER RAITA

The perfect dip for those freshly cooked pakora's and bhajia's.

**SERVES 4**

## INGREDIENTS

- *100g coriander*
- *1 green chilli*
- *1 garlic*
- *200g Greek yogurt*
- *Salt, to taste*

## METHOD

In a blender, blend the coriander, green chilli and garlic into a smooth paste. Stir in the Greek yogurt and season with salt.

# DARNA LASARN CHUTNEY (GARLIC AND CORIANDER CHUTNEY)

I like to keep this in my fridge for up to 4 weeks. When I fancy a quick tasty snack that I like to use it as a spread. The chutney goes well with sandwiches, toast or simply spread over a chapati and then roll it up.

**SERVES 4**

### INGREDIENTS

- *100g finely chopped coriander*
- *3 garlic cloves*
- *1 green chilli*
- *Pinch of salt*
- *Squeeze of lemon*
- *¼ Tsp of oil*

### METHOD

In a blender, add the coriander, garlic, green chilli and salt. Grind to a pulp. Add a squeeze of lemon juice and add a tsp of oil. The oil will keep the chutney fresh and help to retain its vibrant green colour. It should last for up to 2 weeks in the fridge.

For a quick snack spread the chutney over chapati, roll it up and enjoy.

# CORIANDER AND CHILLI RAITA

Coriander is fundamental to almost every dish. I can be a little over generous with it, as this side complements any platter.

**SERVES 4-6**

### INGREDIENTS

- *150g of chopped coriander*
- *250g Greek yogurt (feel free to use fat free)*
- *½ tsp green chilli paste*
- *Juice of ½ lime*
- *Salt, to taste*

### METHOD

In a blender, blend all the above ingredients. Add a couple of teaspoons of water if it's too thick. Make sure not to make it too runny.

# CARROT AND CUCUMBER RAITA

This is the perfect accompaniment to a rice dish!

**SERVES 4**

### INGREDIENTS

- *1 cucumber*
- *1 carrot*
- *½ tsp garlic paste*
- *1 tsp green chilli paste*
- *1 tsp ground cumin*
- *1 tsp salt*
- *400g approx. set/hung yogurt*

### METHOD

In a large mixing bowl grate the cucumber with a cheese grater. Place the cucumber into a muslin cloth and squeeze all the water from the cucumber. Transfer the cucumber back to the mixing bowl and grate in the carrot too. Add the remaining ingredients including the yogurt. Combine and mix all the ingredients together. This will stay in an airtight container in the fridge for 2 days.

This raita is the perfect accompaniment to many of my dishes in this book, in particular my Dal Bhat *(page 48)*.

# MANGO AND MINT CHUTNEY

A fresh and vibrantly spiced chutney balanced with the sweetness from the mango.

**SERVES 4-6**

### INGREDIENTS

- *1 ripe large mango*
- *20g mint leaves*
- *1 inch piece ginger*
- *¼ tsp rock salt*
- *1 red birds eye chilli*
- *¼ tsp cumin powder*

### METHOD

Add all the listed ingredients to a blender and blend to silky smooth puree. Garnish with little chunks of mango and serve with papadoms or paratha. This will store in the fridge for 3-4 days

# CREAMY AVOCADO RAITA

Emulsify an avocado into a mix of flavours to bring freshness to the table, with a kick of chilli and lime. Serve it as a side and it is guaranteed to enhance your dish.

**SERVES 4-6**

## INGREDIENTS

- *1 large avocado*
- *½ tsp garlic paste*
- *½ tsp green chilli paste*
- *¼ tsp ground cumin*
- *Juice of 2 limes*
- *Zest of 1 lime*
- *250g Greek yogurt (feel free to use fat free)*
- *1 tbsp fresh coriander, finely chopped*
- *Salt, to taste*

## METHOD

In a bowl mix together all the above ingredients. Blend with a hand blender or a masher to keep a few chunks of the avocado in the raita for texture.

Goes great papadums or toasted pitta breads.

# SWEET TREATS

# SEERO/ SOOJI HALWA (SEMOLINA HALWA)

This is a quick sweet dish made with semolina. I have grown up eating this sweet dish. It was one of my favourite things. In fact, it was every Indian kids favourite sweet. It was made at all auspicious occasions, but also whenever we would fancy it. Most people love a bowl of soup when they have the sniffles, however, I love a bowl of delicious seero. It's filling, warming, soothing and gives you the lift that you need when you're feeling low. I mean you don't have to be poorly to have a bowl of seero, any excuse will do. You're in for a treat with this one.

**SERVES 2**

## INGREDIENTS

- *125g fine white semolina*
- *55ml melted ghee*
- *½ tsp ground cardamom*
- *2 tbsp unsalted cashew halves*
- *2 tbsp raisins*
- *1 tbsp pistachios, finely chopped*
- *1 tbsp almonds, finely chopped*
- *280ml warm milk*
- *5 tsp granulated sugar*
- *Saffron for decoration.*

## METHOD

In a heavy bottom wide saucepan, melt the ghee on a low heat and add the semolina. Gently bake in the pan continuously stirring. When you can see the ghee starting to come away and separate from the semolina add the cashews and raisins and mix well. Now add the warm milk gradually while stirring the semolina. Now add the cardamom and sugar. Combine all the ingredients together well. Stirring often, cook until the ghee starts to separate at the edges again. Take off the heat and serve with garnishing's of finely chopped pistachios and almonds. To add that final flourish of decadence, add a few strands of saffron. Serve while its warm, it will melt in your mouth.

# CHAI-SPICED BREAD AND BUTTER PUDDING

A twist on a classic with rich buttery brioche and custard infused with chai spices. A timeless classic with the flavours of India.

**SERVES 4**

## INGREDIENTS

- *6 slices of brioche bread*
- *2 tbsp butter*
- *3 medium eggs*
- *400ml milk*
- *200g jaggery, finely chopped*
- *2 tsp loose tea*
- *7-8 cardamom pods*
- *2-3 cloves*
- *2 peppercorns*
- *1 inch cinnamon stick*
- *½ tsp ground nutmeg*
- *1 tsp ginger, grated*
- *100g dried fruit (I use raisins, cranberries and apricot)*

## METHOD

Prepare the chai milk but placing a medium sized saucepan on medium heat with the milk, loose tea, cardamom pods, cloves, peppercorns, cinnamon stick, ground nutmeg and ginger. Bring to boil, then simmer on a low heat for a further 5 minutes. Take off the heat, allow the chai milk to settle for 2-3 minutes then stir in the jaggery. Allow the chai milk to cool for 15-20 minutes.

Pre heat your oven to 170c.

Grease an oven safe baking dish (8x8) with butter.

Butter the slices of brioche bread of both sides, cut into triangles and arrange in overlapping rows in the greased baking dish.

If your chai milk has cooled down, you can now whisk all 3 eggs in. Pour this into the dish over your buttered brioche.

Place in the oven and bake for approx. 40-45 minutes. When ready it will be puffed and golden. Serve warm with vanilla custard.

MANGO AND COCONUT BARFI

# MANGO AND COCONUT BARFI

A soft melt in the mouth barfi with a fudgy texture and the sweetness of mangos, it makes the perfect end to any meal. The perfect tropical flavour combo that everyone will love.

**MAKES APPROX 12 SERVINGS**

## INGREDIENTS

- *400g desiccated coconut*
- *400ml full fat milk*
- *200ml tinned mango pulp*
- *200g granulated sugar*
- *10 strands of saffron*
- *2 tbsp almonds flakes*

## METHOD

Place a heavy bottom saucepan on medium-high heat. Add desiccated coconut, milk, mango pump and sugar. Stir everything together well. Continuously stir on a medium-high heat for 15 minutes at which point you will start to see the mixture thicken and the colour turn from yellow to orange.

Turn the heat down to medium heat and add the saffron. Continue to stir for a further 5 mins. As the mixture starts to turn a dough, lower the heat to low and cook for another 5-7 minutes stirring continuously.

Take off the heat and transfer the mixture to a tin lined with parchment paper. Smooth out with a spatula forming a layer approx. 1 inch thick. Garnish with almond flakes, pressing them into the barfi gently.

Place in the fridge for 2 hours to set.

Cut into 12 equal square pieces and serve.

Store in an airtight container in the fridge for up to 2 weeks.

# WHITE BARFI

A very popular Indian sweet fudge recipe which is gluten free and a no bake dessert. It's usually a sweet prepared during Indian festivals or special occasions, although, for me any day calls for barfi! There are so many different varieties of barfi, but I'm keeping this plain and simple as it's my favourite. The barfi melts in your mouth.

**MAKES APPROX 12 SERVINGS**

## INGREDIENTS

- *500g milk powder*
- *100g granulated sugar*
- *50g melted ghee*
- *150ml full fat milk*
- *¼ tsp ground cardamom*
- *2 tbsp almonds, finely chopped*
- *2 tbsp pistachios, finely chopped*

## METHOD

Heat a large saucepan on low heat. Add the melted ghee, milk, milk powder and granulated sugar. Mix well and stir continuously. The sugar should start to melt. Continue to stir on a low heat and you will start to see the milk thicken gradually. Continue stirring for a further 8-10 minutes until a dough starts to form. Careful not overcook otherwise it will become chewy. Add the ground cardamom and mix well. Take off the heat.

Transfer the barfi dough to a greased tin lined with parchment paper. Smooth out with a spatula and form an inch thick block. Sprinkle with the finely chopped almonds and pistachios. Press them lightly into the barfi. Allow the barfi to set for 2 hours, until it is completely set.

Remove from the tin and cut into 12 equal square pieces.

Store in an airtight container for up to 2 weeks.

# GULAB JAMUN CAKES

Gulab Jamun is a quintessential classic Indian dessert. It is the queen of all Indian desserts. I've transformed a classic dessert into cake. The perfect accompaniment to you afternoon cup of chai. A cupcake or 2 will surely make you close your eyes and enter a state of pure heaven.

**MAKES 24 SERVINGS**

## INGREDIENTS

- *200g self raising flour*
- *100g caster sugar*
- *50g milk powder*
- *2 tsp baking powder*
- *1 tbsp crushed almonds*
- *1 tbsp crushed pistachios*
- *1 tbsp fine white semolina*
- *1 tbsp desiccated coconut*
- *4-5 strand saffron*
- *¼ tsp grated nutmeg*
- *½ tsp ground cardamom*
- *250ml plain Greek yogurt*
- *3 tbsp milk*
- *5 tbsp sunflower oil*
- *Chopped pistachios for decoration*
- *Edible dried rose petals for decoration*

## METHOD

Start to preheat your oven at 180c

In a mixing bowl add the plain Greek yogurt, milk and sunflower oil. Whisk them together and keep aside.

In another mixing bowl, sift the self-raising flour and baking powder. Add the caster sugar and milk powder. Mix in the semolina, desiccated coconut, saffron strands, cardamom powder, nutmeg, and crushed pistachios and almonds. To this bowl add the whisked yogurt and fold all the ingredients together gently to make the gulab jamun cake mixture.

Grease a mini cupcake baking tray or line with mini cupcake cases. Scoop 1 tbsp of the gulab jamun cake mixture into each of the cases. Sprinkle with chopped pistachios and place in the oven for 15 mins until fully baked, or until a toothpick comes out clean when inserted in the middle of the cakes.

Cool on a wire rack and sprinkle with edible rose petals.

# ROSE AND BERRY ETON MESS

A simple twist on the classic Eton mess. My rose syrup and cardamom scented version is easy to put together for a last minute craving.

## INGREDIENTS

- *4 meringue nests*
- *250ml double cream*
- *150g strawberries*
- *150g raspberries*
- *Tsp fresh lemon juice*
- *4 tbsp rose syrup*
- *¼ tsp ground cardamom*
- *2 tbsp roughly chopped pistachios*

## METHOD

In a mixing bowl whip the double cream until smooth and peaks form. Gently fold in the ground cardamom.

Take half of the strawberries and half of the raspberries in a separate bowl, add the rose syrup and lemon juice. I use a hand blender to blend everything together.

Slice the remaining strawberries. Leave the remaining raspberries whole.

Add the blended berries to the bowl of whipped cream. Break up the meringue nests into large bitesize chunks and add them to the bowl of berries and cream. Add the sliced strawberries and raspberries.

Gently fold together the contents of the bowl to create a marbled effect.

Transfer to serving bowls/plates with a scattering of pistachios.

# FRUIT SALAD

A delicious creamy and chilled dessert made with custard powder, milk, nut and seasonal fruit. This is a popular dessert in India and I have so many memories of this growing up. I remember helping my dad chop all the fruits for this mouth-watering dessert. Each fruit had to be sliced in a certain way. It was a joint family effort but of so worth it. The best thing is it doesn't haven't to be just for dessert, you can have it any time of the day.

**SERVES 2**

## INGREDIENTS

- *500ml full fat milk + 100ml*
- *3 tbsp Custard powder*
- *100g sugar*
- *Seasonal Fruit – Apples, Pears, Bananas, grapes, pomegranate, mango*
- *Cashews*
- *Roughly ground cardamom*

## METHOD

In saucepan on medium heat at 500ml milk and bring to boil. Turn the heat down to low and add the sugar. Simmer on a low heat until the sugar dissolves. In separate cup, mix the custard powder with 100ml of cold milk. Add this mix to the simmering milk. Keep stirring continuously. Simmer for a further 5 minutes until the raw smell of custard begins to fade. Take off the heat and place in the saucepan of custard milk in a sink of cold water (ensuring none of water goes into the saucepan). Cool down the custard milk until it's room temperature. Now add the roughly ground cardamom, stir well and place in the fridge. Meanwhile you can chop your fruits. Avoid watery/juicy fruits like watermelon/oranges. Add your chopped fruits and cashews to the cooling custard milk in the fridge. Stir and combine well. Keep in the fridge for a few hours before serving. Makes a delicious and filling cooling snack or dessert.

# MANGO SHRIKHAND CHEESECAKES

Mouth watering mini mango skrikhand cheesecakes. The creaminess comes from the yogurt and fresh mango pulp, and a touch of luxuriousness of saffron, cardamom and nutmeg. Shrikhand is normally made by straining yogurt, however this is my quick fix delicious version.

**SERVES 6**

## INGREDIENTS

- *100g ginger nut biscuits*
- *1 ½ tbsp unsalted butter*
- *50g almonds, roughly chopped*
- *50g pistachios, roughly chopped*
- *200g mascarpone*
- *100g cream cheese*
- *200g Greek yogurt*
- *6 tbsp icing sugar*
- *Pinch of grated nutmeg*
- *½ tsp ground cardamom*
- *4-5 strands saffron dissolved in 1 tbsp warm milk*
- *1 mango, peeled and destoned and blended to a pulp*
- *Almond and pistachio slivers for garnish*
- *Mint leaves for garnish*

## METHOD

In a food processor blend the ginger biscuits with the butter until you have a ginger crumb mixture.

In a mixing bowl whisk together the mascarpone, cream cheese and Greek yogurt. Whisk until combined and fluffy. Whisk in the saffron-milk mix, nutmeg and cardamom powder. Gently mix in the icing sugar. Fold in the chopped almonds and pistachios. The shrikhand filling is ready.

In 6 small glass/cups, distribute the ginger biscuit crumb into the bottom of each glass. Use the back of a spoon to press down lightly. Now evenly distribute a layer of shrikhand filling into each of the glasses.

Add a thin layer of mango pulp on top of the shrikhand. Garnish with Almond and Pistachio slivers, and mint leaves.

Leave to chill in the fridge for 2 hours +, until the mango sets on top before serving and enjoy.

# GAJAR HALWA (CARROT PUDDING)

This is normally a very rich and exotic dessert made with copious amounts of ghee, sugar and condensed milk or khoya. It's mostly enjoyed at weddings and Diwali. However, my recipe is a lighter version of the classic gajar halwa that can be enjoyed whatever the occasion! Have this with a scoop of good quality vanilla ice cream – you'll be in heaven.

**SERVES 4-6**

## INGREDIENTS

- *500g of carrots, peeled and grated with a fine grater*
- *500ml of whole milk*
- *3 tbsp ghee*
- *50g granulated sugar*
- *½ tsp ground cardamom*
- *1 tbsp chopped almonds*
- *1 tbsp chopped cashews*
- *2 tbsp raisins, for decoration*
- *1 tbsp pistachios chopped, for decoration*

## METHOD

Heat the ghee in a heavy bottom saucepan on medium heat. Add the chopped almonds and cashews, and fry them until they turn golden. Set them aside on some tissue paper. In the same ghee add the grated carrots to the pan. Sauté well for approx. 5 minutes until it changes colour slightly. Now pour in the milk, stir continuously and bring to boil. Reduce the heat right down and simmer for 40-50 minutes, stirring often to avoid it sticking to the bottom of the pan. At this point the milk will have reduced significantly and carrots will be soft and delicate. Add the sugar and continue to cook on a low heat until all the sugar has dissolved, and the ghee rises to the top of the mixture. Turn the heat off now, add the ground cardamom, the fried almonds and cashews, and gently stir through. Serve with scatterings of chopped pistachios and raisins, and a scoop of vanilla ice cream. Delectably divine.

# SNACKS AND NIBBLES

# PEANUT AND SEA SALT CHIKKI

A traditional Indian sweet candy made with jaggery and peanuts or sesame seeds. The whole family will love them. Here is an easy way to make this moreish delicacy. My children like to coat theirs in melted chocolate and sprinkles. Fun for the whole family.

**MAKES APPROX 12 SERVINGS**

## INGREDIENTS

- *180g roasted, skinless plain peanuts*
- *100g jaggery*
- *1 tbsp water*
- *¼ tsp sea salt*

## METHOD

Place a saucepan on low heat to which add the jaggery and water. Melt the jaggery until it starts to bubble. Continue to stir for a few minutes until it turns to a syrup. Add a small drop of the syrup to a glass of cold water. It should solidify. At this point you can add the roasted plain peanuts to the saucepan. Mix well to evenly coat the peanuts. Stir in the sea salt. Take off the heat and pour over some grease proof paper. Place another piece of greaseproof paper over the top and roll the chikki mixture to approx. 1cm in thickness.

Let this completely cool before cutting into 2-inch squared pieces. Store in an airtight container.

# CHANA DAL CHAAT

Baked chana dal tossed in spices and onions. A delicious accompaniment with your tipple of choice.

**SERVES 2**

## INGREDIENTS

- *200g split chana dal, soaked overnight*
- *½ tsp red chilli powder*
- *1 tsp salt, or to taste*
- *2 green chillies, finely chopped*
- *1 red onion, finely chopped*
- *Juice of ½ lemon*
- *3 tbsp finely chopped coriander*
- *75g mild cheddar cheese, cut into 5mm cubes*

## METHOD

Firstly, drain the chana dal and pat completely dry with kitchen paper. Transfer the chana dal to a mixing bowl to which add the red chilli powder and salt.

Spread the chana dal onto a lined baking tray and roast in a preheated oven of 160 degrees for approx. 35-40. Once cooked, allow cool the chana dal.

Transfer the roasted chana dal to a large mixing bowl, add the finely chopped red onion, green chillies, lemon juice, coriander and mild cheddar.

Toss all the ingredients together.

Serve with your favourite tipple of choice. A crowd pleaser for sure!

# MASALA PAPADUM

An easy appetiser of crunchy papadums topped with a crunchy and fresh masala salad. Perfect with an ice-cold beer under the summer sun.

**SERVES 2**

## INGREDIENTS

- *2 plain papadums*
- *1 red onion, finely chopped*
- *1 tomato, finely chopped*
- *2 tbsp fresh coriander, finely chopped*
- *1 tsp red chilli powder*
- *1 tsp fresh lime juice*
- *¼ tsp salt, or to taste*
- *Sunflower oil for deep frying*

## METHOD

In a frying pan, heat sunflower oil on a low heat to 180 degrees for deep frying. Fry the papadoms for a few seconds on each side until crisp. Drain on kitchen tissue paper.

Transfer the fried papadoms to a serving dish. Evenly sprinkle each papadom with the finely chopped onions and tomatoes. Sprinkle over the chilli powder and salt. Drizzle over the lime juice and garnish with fresh coriander.

Serve immediately otherwise they will turn soggy.

# FRUIT AND NUT CHIKKI

A traditional Indian brittle bar with so many variations to satisfy your sweet tooth. Loaded with dry fruit, mixed nuts, healthy seeds and iron rich jaggery. A quick breakfast on the go, or the perfect midday energy boosting snack.

**MAKES APPROX 20 SERVINGS**

## INGREDIENTS

- *100g unsalted cashews, halved*
- *100g unsalted almonds, halved*
- *30g unsalted pistachios*
- *50g raisins and dry cranberries*
- *30g pumpkin seeds*
- *200g jaggery*
- *1 ¼ tsp ghee*
- *¼ tsp cardamom powder*
- *50ml warm water*

## METHOD

Firstly, dry roast the nuts (cashews, almonds, pistachios) in a wide frying pan on low heat, stirring often. Roast until they turn crunchy. Do not burn them. Transfer to a bowl and set to one side.

In the same frying pan, on low heat, add the warm water with the jaggery and ghee. Stir continuously until the jaggery dissolves. Bring to boil, stirring often for 5 minutes. You will see it start to form a froth. To check the syrup is ready, drip a small drop of the syrup into a glass of cold water. It should harden instantly with the ability to snap/crush it. If not, boil the syrup for another minute or so until you reach the desired consistency. Now add the roasted nuts, raisins and dry cranberries, and the cardamom powder. Combine everything together well. take off the heat and quickly transfer to grease proof paper. Cover with another piece of grease proof paper on top and roll the chikki mix. Roll quickly, but evenly to a 1cm in thickness. Remove the top layer of grease proof paper and allow the chikki to cool slightly for a couple of minutes. Cut into 20 equal pieces, careful not burn your fingers. Once cut, cool completely and serve. Store in an airtight container for up to 3 weeks.

# SPICY CASHEWS (THE PERFECT SNACK WITH A BEER!)

They are spicy, mouth burning, but so so moreish. You'll keep going back for more. This was my dads go to snack he'd make when he had family and friends over for drinks.

**SERVES 2**

## INGREDIENTS

- *200g salted cashews*
- *½ tsp red chilli powder*
- *½ tsp sunflower oil*

## METHOD

In a wok/frying pan, heat the oil on a medium heat and add the salted cashews. Toss the cashews around the pan with the oil. Careful to keep the cashews whole. Toast the cashews for 5 minutes stirring often. Add the red chilli powder. You can add more if you want more spice. Coat the cashews well in the chilli powder and cook for a further 10 minutes. Serve as the perfect nibble with an ice cold beer.

# DRINKS

MASALA CHAI

# MASALA CHAI

Enjoyed by millions in India and all over the world, masala chai is a spiced, sweetened black tea mixed with milk which is aromatic, warming and simply beautiful. Everyone has their own ways and versions of making masala chai. I have grown up with the version. In fact, my dad taught me to me make my very first cup of chai.

**SERVES 2**

## INGREDIENTS

- *200ml water*
- *4 tsp granulated sugar*
- *3 tsp loose tea*
- *¼ tsp coarsely ground cardamom seeds*
- *½ tsp chai masala*
- *½ inch freshly grated ginger (grate with the skin on)*
- *2 sprigs of mint leaves*
- *1 tsp dried lemongrass (optional)*
- *300ml milk*

## METHOD

In a large saucepan/milk pan add the water along with all the other ingredients apart from the milk.

Place the pan on a high heat and bring to boil. Continue to boil for 2 minutes so all the aromatics infuse the water. Now turn the heat down to low and pour in the milk. Turn the heat up to high again and bring to boil. You need to keep an eye on it, otherwise the chai with overflow as it comes to boil. As soon as you start to see the chai raising to surface of the pan, turn the heat right down to low.

Now simmer on a low heat for a further 5 minutes.

Take of the heat and strain the chai into mugs.

Enjoy the soothing, warming complexities that this mug of chai will bring you.

# DESI CAPPUCCINO

Such a simple coffee recipe that will have you coming back for more. This is a rich, creamy and frothy coffee with the warming taste of cardamom. I am a regular coffee drinker, but I like to drink this during the evening.

**SERVES 2**

## INGREDIENTS

- *400ml milk*
- *2 ½ tsp granulated sugar*
- *2 tsp instant coffee granules*
- *2-3 cardamon pods, ground*

## METHOD

In a saucepan on medium heat, bring 400ml of milk to boil. Turn the heat down to low, add the sugar, coffee and ground cardamom and stir gently. Simmer for 2 minutes on a low heat. Pour into 2 cups and enjoy.

# GINGERBREAD AND CARDAMOM HOT CHOCOLATE

I am addicted to this drink. Perfect for those cosey nights under the duvet and a crowd pleaser for sure!

**SERVES 2**

## INGREDIENTS

- *500ml milk (full fat or semi-skimmed) + 3 tbsp*
- *125g dark chocolate (min 70% cocoa)*
- *1 tbsp cocoa powder*
- *1 tsp light brown sugar*
- *1 tsp ground cardamom (freshly ground if possible)*
- *1 tbsp gingerbread syrup*

### Optional Ingredients:

- *Squirty cream*
- *Marshmallows*
- *Grated chocolate*

## METHOD

In a cup whisk together 3 tbsp of cold milk with 1 tbsp of cocoa powder until you have a smooth paste.

In a heavy bottom saucepan heat 250ml of milk and simmer on a medium-low heat.

Add the cocoa paste and stir into the milk.

Now add the dark chocolate. Allow it to melt on a low heat, continue to stir.

Add the remaining milk, light brown sugar, ground cardamom and ginger syrup.

Using a whisk, mix the ingredients together and continue to simmer and gently whisk on a low heat for a minute. Do not bring to boil otherwise the milk will form a layer of skin.

Remove from the heat and serve in your favourite mug. Bring out the inner child in you by topping with squirty cream, marshmallows and grated chocolate.

# BADAM PISTA DHOOD

This is your Indian version of a warm malted milk drink. Ground almonds and pistachios mixed with warming spices to create a warming drink which can be soothing on a cold winter's day, as it's rich, filling and satisfying. Before energy drinks were invented, this natural form of a pick-me-up drink was created!

**SERVES 2**

## INGREDIENTS

- *2 tbsp almonds*
- *1 tbsp pistachios*
- *¾ tsp freshly ground cardamom pods*
- *4-5 strand saffron*
- *400ml milk (I normally use semi-skimmed) – feel free to use any milk/milk substitute*
- *2 ½ - 3tsp Granulated sugar*

## METHOD

In a saucepan gently heat the milk on medium heat. Meanwhile, using a pestle and mortar, pound the nuts to a grainy, semi-ground texture.

Bring the milk to a gentle boil, and add the semi ground pistachios and almonds, sugar and ground cardamom. Mix well into the milk

Turn the heat down to low and simmer. Add the saffron and stir through milk. Simmer for a further minute.

Pour into your mug and enjoy.

# MASALA CHAAS/MATHO (SPICED BUTTERMILK)

Masala Chaas is a popular Indian yogurt drink, also known as spiced buttermilk, it is made with yogurt, water and some spices. This poured over Kichdi or vegetable rice is perfect on a hot summer day to cool you down. This reminds me of those hot blazing days when I wanted Indian food, but nothing too warm. There are Indians who like to drink this straight over ice. I say each to their own.

**SERVES 4**

## INGREDIENTS

- *245g yogurt*
- *350ml water*
- *1 clove garlic*
- *1 green chilli*
- *½ tsp granulated sugar*
- *¼ tsp ground cumin*
- *¼ tsp salt , or to taste*
- *Chopped fresh coriander for garnish*
- *Fresh mint leaves for garnish*

## METHOD

In a pitcher whisk together the yogurt, granulated sugar, cumin powder and salt. Blend the garlic and green chilli into a paste and add to the pitcher. Add the water and whisk for 3-4 minutes until you form a froth on the surface of the chaas. Gently swirl in the chopped coriander and mint leaves.

Pour into glasses and serve simply as a cooling drink. Also tastes divine poured over khichdi with any of my ravaiya recipes.

# NIMBU PANI

This jazzed up lemon water is thirst quenching on a hot summer's day! My dad would always make this for us. His nimbu pani was the best because he'd always put a cheeky extra spoon of sugar in for us. You can adjust the sweetness of this drink to your taste. A winner with the whole family.

**SERVES 4**

## INGREDIENTS

- *2 lemons + extra lemon slices for garnish*
- *1150ml ice cold water*
- *6 tbsp granulated sugar*
- *Handful of mint leaves + extra for garnish*

## METHOD

Blend the mint leaves and granulated sugar in a blender to create a course mixture. In a large pitcher add the juice from 2 lemons and ground sugar and mint mix. Pour in 1 pint of water and continuously stir until the sugar dissolves in the water. Add the remaining 1 pint of water. Stir well and add a few slices of lemon and mint leaves into the pitcher as a garnish.

Pour over ice into glasses. A super refreshing, thirst quenching summer drink.

Milton Keynes UK
Ingram Content Group UK Ltd.
UKHW050132290724
446136UK00004B/59

9 781913 568634